PASOLD OCCASIONAL PAPERS

General Editor: K. G. PONTING

VOLUME I

A PRACTICAL TREATISE ON DYING

By William Partridge

Originally published in 1823

This edition edited by K. G. Ponting (1973)

VOLUME 2

EMPLOYER AND EMPLOYED

Ford, Ayrton & Co. Ltd, Silk Spinners

By Elizabeth R. and John H. P. Pafford

Employer and Employed

FORD, AYRTON & CO. LTD
SILK SPINNERS

With Worker Participation

LEEDS and LOW BENTHAM

1870 - 1970

By

ELIZABETH R. PAFFORD
and JOHN H. P. PAFFORD

PASOLD RESEARCH FUND LTD
Edington, Wiltshire

1974

'In this mill one of the most interesting experiments ever attempted in industrial relations is being carried out and is proving a success that may have far-reaching effects in the industrial world of the future.'

(*The Yorkshire Evening News*, 15 June 1933
See Book List 24)

'At a time when industrial harmony is the greatest need of the country, this successful venture would seem to indicate the path to understanding.'

(*Town and Country News*, 8 April 1927
See Book List 22)

'These things cannot be done without sacrifice, not only material but also the love of power over other men's lives which is in all of us. The feeling of complete ownership must give way to a sense of sharing in all things.'

(Charles Ford, *See* p. 50)

PRINTED IN GREAT BRITAIN BY W. S. MANEY AND SON LTD LEEDS

INTRODUCTORY NOTE

Amongst its historical interests the Pasold Research Fund is particularly concerned to play a part in the preservation and publication of business records. For this reason it is happy to publish as its second Occasional Paper *Employer and Employed* by Elizabeth R. and John H. P. Pafford. Ford, Ayrton were well known in the textile trade as silk spinners and they have a special interest at the present time because of their successful application of co-partnership and profit-sharing. Mrs Pafford is the daughter of the last member of the family to be in charge of the business. Dr Pafford, for many years Goldsmiths' Librarian of the University of London, himself became chairman during the last years of the firm's life.

In addition to the interest in the scheme for worker participation and the fact that the firm was the last to carry out the whole process of silk spinning in England, this volume shows how important it is that histories of small as well as of large firms should be published.

K.G.P.

CONTENTS

ILLUSTRATIONS

PREFACE

IN 1971 we wrote to Tom Bownass[1] telling him of this projected account of Ford, Ayrton and asking a few questions. Barely two months later we received from him a history of the mill and the Ford family. That it was not quite of the kind we had in mind is neither here nor there: it was a remarkable and most helpful achievement. And since then, in correspondence and in person, he has been unfailingly helpful. No less great is our debt to Will Hawkins who has given much information both by letter and in person: both he and Tom Bownass read the typescript and have saved us from many errors and omissions. We are also indebted to Eleanor and Ursula Ford for reading the typescript and for helpful comments.

Valuable information has been obtained from a short unpublished history of the mill written by Charles Ford in September 1961 and from other of his unpublished letters and papers, and, of course, from personal knowledge of his views on the mill. Similar information has come from personal contacts we have had over the years with many who served the mill. Perhaps the chief of these is Will Bruce. His recollections of the mill, recorded on tape by Dr Leslie Dowell, have been most useful as have also his personal answers to our queries.

A main source of information has naturally been the Company's books and documents. When the mill closed these were transferred to the Leeds City Archives where they are housed at the Sheepscar branch of the City Libraries. We are indebted to Mr J. M. Collinson, City Archivist, not only for giving us every facility to use them but for himself kindly checking them to answer our enquiries. Compared with those of many firms now closed the surviving records of Ford, Ayrton are extensive although, of course, not complete. The Company's Minutes for 19 June 1940 show that some went in

[1] The index will give further references to many people named.

the drive for waste-paper in the second war: 'Messrs Titus
Wilson & Son of Kendal had asked if we had any old papers or
books to dispose of. It was agreed to . . . dispose of all old
books except wages Books and Ledgers and all old correspondence and receipts and other papers more than 6 years
old.'

Most of the published material used is recorded in the Book
List on pages 69–73, which gives fuller details of works men-
tioned in the text. The list has been kindly checked by Mr
P. A. Townhill.

We are indebted to the University of London Library and
particularly, among its staff, to Miss M. J. Canney and Mr
A. H. Wesencraft. Many persons and firms have given information or lent books, and some have generously given their
publications – as Messrs Brocklehurst Fabrics Ltd (Mr J. W.
Warren), and H. T. Gaddum & Co. Ltd (Mr Peter Gaddum),
each of Macclesfield, and J., T. & J. Taylor, Ltd (Mr Sam B.
Stokes) of Batley. Through the kind offices of Sir Ernest
Goodale, Messrs Warner and Sons, Ltd gave us an extended
loan of Sir Frank Warner's book on the silk industry; and Mr
Ian Gordon-Brown, Director of the Industrial Participation
(formerly Co-Partnership) Association, gave information and
loan of books.

We are greatly indebted to all who have helped but are, of
course, ourselves entirely responsible for all opinions expressed
and for all shortcomings in the book.

E.R.P.

Bridport, 24 January 1974   J.H.P.P.

I

Introduction

THIS IS IN outline the story of Ford, Ayrton & Co. Ltd, Silk
Spinners, a small Yorkshire family business which began in
Leeds in 1870 and closed in Bentham in 1970. It is not primarily
a technical book but concentrates more on the personalities and
principles of some of those who founded and managed the mill
and on some others who worked in it, and on the profit-sharing,
co-partnership and other schemes which were introduced to
bring employees into participation with the management in the
policy and working of the mill and to share in its profits. In
these matters, and particularly in the spirit in which they were
conceived and operated, Ford, Ayrton is believed to have
differed in some ways which are of interest from other silk
spinning concerns, whereas on the technical side the firm may
have had little to show which was not common practice in the
trade.

Nevertheless it is hoped that enough is said to give the
general reader some idea of the history of silk spinning and of
the nature and production of waste silk, of its processing into
silk yarn and of its uses. But the book does not go closely into
detail and is intended more for the layman than for the technical, economic or historical expert.

During its ninety-three years in Bentham, Ford, Ayrton was
the only industry in a fairly small village — population about
800. The firm and the village therefore meant much to each
other: it could almost be said — particularly of the earlier days,
before radio, television, and easy communications and travel
— that they formed a community, and certainly the manage-

ment of the mill worked and lived as part of the village. A full
appreciation of what this meant could only be given by someone
who had entered into the lives and homes of those who worked
in the mill, and had been able to do so over a long period of
time. Manifestly this would have been impossible; but to those
who managed the mill, and to many, and perhaps to all, who
worked in it, this sense of a mill/village community was something that mattered. It was also the result of completely natural
growth. There was nothing artificial, never any attempt by the
Ford family to set up a model village of any kind: they would
not have been rich enough, but certainly would never have had
this intention. Their social position and influence would make
an interesting feature in a study of the fascinating subject of
village life. For, as with many English villages, although there
were large and important areas of co-operation, as in parish
council, social, sporting and other activities, Bentham in the
Fords' time — at any rate up to 1914 — was also divided
into 'Church' and 'Chapel'. To over-simplify — the Church
element usually included most of the 'gentry' and their depen-
dents, and farmers, and was Conservative; and Chapel most of
the industrialists and the less well off generally, and was Liberal/
Labour. In Bentham there were few who could have been
termed landed gentry, and the Fords, although non-conformist
and Liberal/Labour, were not exactly Chapel: they were of the
very small Quaker community. But they supported Church,
Chapel, schools, social, sporting activities and indeed anything
that seemed worth while in the village, and so were to some
extent an independent and unifying element in village life.

And the story of the mill itself, small as it was — the maximum number of workers at one time was about 230, and over
the years the average at any one time was probably little over
100 — may have something to offer in the field of industrial
relations. For in this matter, one of the greatest and most
important problems of our day, it had an excellent record
throughout its history. Life in the mill was normal, healthy,
robust mill life. There were the personal likes and dislikes and

the occasional quarrels natural in any organization, but there was also overall harmony and goodwill and plenty of happiness and fun.

It may be that the smallness of the firm and of the village is one main reason why the whole enterprise — the profit-sharing, and co-partnership and allied schemes, the industrial relations and the mill/village 'community' — was successful. Certainly it is hard to imagine a corresponding spirit of unity in a big firm, one of many in a large city. Indeed any similar achievement, as a whole, would in those circumstances obviously be impossible. This is, of course, by no means to say that profit-sharing, co-partnership and other participation schemes would not succeed, or even that they would be less likely to do so, in a large firm in an industrial city. There is plenty of proof that this is not so. What the Ford, Ayrton story may show is the extent and depth to which a small firm in a small community can promote prosperity and happiness and still be a commercial success; for it must be noted that the firm held out against foreign competition longer than all others in its field: it was the last British silk-spinning mill wholly and fully concerned with the business. And so, while it is true that no other silk-spinning mill was large, Ford, Ayrton may also have something to offer on the possibilities of commercial success by small undertakings, however liberal their attitude to employees, and indeed perhaps because of that attitude. Like many others, the mill was a community: but unlike some, there was no remoteness in control, but the precise opposite. There was integration; for workers shared in the management; and relationship between management and workers — where practically all the management were employed in the mill and some in the processing rooms — was close, free and open. From 1919 onwards full information about the firm's policy and activities, trading position and finances was always directly available to all workers who were shareholders. Important results of this were general awareness of what all were thinking about the mill and knowledge that all could have a personal say as well as function in it.

There was indeed not only no remoteness in control, there was none between any shareholder and the mill. For all shareholders were either working in the mill or actively concerned in its management — and these held almost all the shares — or else were very close relatives of those who were doing so. At all times in its history every shareholder knew the mill and most of them were part of its immediate community — the one partial exception was a widow of a Director, Mrs Robert Ayrton senior, who died aged 101 in 1962. Furthermore there was no outside traffic in shares. They were never on public offer and everyone knew that no profit could be made on them: until liquidation all transactions were always at par.

But here again it must be said that just as the book is non-technical so it also has no claim to authority in the economics of textile history or the philosophy of industrial relations. It is a non-professional story of one firm and is no doubt coloured by family piety. The writers are also aware that Ford, Ayrton was not the only pebble on the beach, and that many accounts have been and many more could be written of other happy and successful family businesses; all making first-hand records of our social and economic history. The story of Ford, Ayrton may provide something of interest in the history and technicalities of British silk spinning, and, because of its account of a successful experiment in employee participation and sharing, may also have interest, and even practical value, for all concerned with this vital matter in British industry. For although ideas and practice concerning participation naturally change and no doubt will continue to do so, there may be permanent elements of value in the Ford, Ayrton scheme, not least in its spirit and purpose. And all will agree with *The Times* heading to its business correspondence of 8 May 1970, 'Worker participation a key issue of the 70s'.

2

The Founders and Owners

particularly Thomas Benson Pease Ford (afterwards referred to as Benson) and his son Rawlinson Charles (afterwards referred to as Charles) — and their objects

THE HISTORY of a firm is the story of those who founded and managed it, and of all who worked in it, of what they did and how they did it, of the place in which they worked, and of their raw materials, processes, plant, end-products and marketing. This would be a complicated, detailed and long story, and since this account of Ford, Ayrton cannot be long, it must be confined to those matters which seem to be of chief importance. We begin with an account of those who founded and managed the mill, and particularly of Benson and Charles and of the spirit which guided their work.

The firm is one of those often described as a family concern, and this family, which founded and primarily managed the business from first to last, was that of Benson Ford. Born in Leeds in 1846, the second son of Robert Lawson and Hannah Ford (née Pease) of Park Square, and later of Adel Grange, he came of an old family which traces its ancestry back to the early fourteenth century. Benson belonged to that branch which, since Hugh Forde of Ford Green, Staffordshire, joined the newly-formed Society of Friends about 1680, has for the most part remained true to the Quaker faith. Educated at Hitchin and Grove House School, Tottenham, Benson was, on leaving school, apprenticed with the engineering firm of Greenwood & Batley, Armley Road, Leeds. On finishing his apprenticeship Mr Greenwood suggested that he should take

up waste silk spinning. Although the industry seems to have
been practised in Britain since just before 1800, its main
development was from about 1850 — it is not mentioned by
G. R. Porter in 1831 (see Book List 52) — and by 1870 the
trade was becoming very prosperous. Mr Greenwood backed
up his sound advice by offering Benson the use of an empty
building near Albion Works (later well known as Hattersley's
Spindle Works) and to sell him machinery on easy terms — and
it may be noted that Ford, Ayrton continued to buy machinery
from Greenwood & Batley long after the move to Bentham.
Benson's father lent him £1,000, and William Harvey, of
another well-known Leeds Quaker family, having joined the
venture, the firm of Ford & Harvey was established in 1870.
The business outgrew the premises and in 1877, Low Mills,
Bentham was bought and the firm was transferred there in
that year as Benson Ford & Co., since William Harvey, not
wishing to leave Leeds, then gave up his partnership.

Benson Ford carried on alone until 1888 when Edward
Ayrton joined the firm, which then took the name of Ford,
Ayrton & Co., by which — with the addition of 'Ltd' in 1909,
when it became a private limited company — it was known
until its closure. Throughout this book it is called Ford,
Ayrton. Benson was an energetic, just and kindly man. A strict
but not stern disciplinarian, he worked hard himself and
expected everyone else to do the same: he was just as quick to
give keen appreciation of a job well done as to condemn sloppy
work. Both he and Charles spent much time in the mill, not
only in checking work but discussing problems, sometimes
personal, with workers. He saw the business not primarily as
something to make profit for himself and his family but as a
trust which he must conscientiously develop for the best
interests of all concerned — employees, management, and
customers. He therefore set out to produce an article of good
quality at a fair price in working conditions which were as
good as he could make them. He had to work hard, often in
difficult times, to maintain this rationalized idealism, but he

PLATE I. The Ford, Ayrton mill at Low Bentham.
Showing on left, rose garden, the cut taking water power to the turbines,
footbridge. Top, the mill allotments. Bottom right, mill cottages

PLATE IIA
Thomas Benson Pease
Ford
1846–1918
The founder

PLATE IIB
Rawlinson Charles Ford
1879–1964

succeeded. He also gave much time to public service and to the Society of Friends. He was a member of the County Council from 1889 until his death in 1918, and after about 1906 went three times a week to Wakefield on Council business. He was on several Council Committees and as Chairman of the Health Committee was largely instrumental in the establishment of the Tuberculosis Sanatorium at Middleton in 1914. As soon as he was established in Low Bentham he set about agitating for a proper water supply and sanitation for the village, opened a Sunday School for young people and Sunday classes for men, became a member of the Board of Guardians and started a village Reading Room and Cricket Club.

The Ford family house — Brook Cottage — was, and the house still is, on the main street in the centre of the village, close to the post office and the few shops, and within less than five minutes walk of the mill. The family was thus very much part of the village, and as everyone in a village knows what everyone else is doing, so all the village would have known of the comings and goings of the Ford family, just as they themselves knew everyone in the village. And this is how Benson wished it to be: both he and Charles always felt it important that anyone on the management staff of the mill should, if possible, be in and of the village. Many mill owners, just as good men as Benson Ford, would have lived in a more pretentious house outside the village, approached by a drive and purposely detached from the mill and its employees. Benson's purpose was precisely the opposite. He and his family, far from seeking detachment, wanted to be fully involved in the mill and the life of its community.

Benson was largely responsible for the building of a village hall, and press cuttings record a 'sale of useful and ornamental articles by Mr. Ford's children' to help raise money for this. There are many records of the family organizing and taking part in village concerts and entertainments, usually to aid good causes, including village activities, such as at least one to raise funds for the cricket club, of which at one time Charles was

2

captain and Gervase a leading batsman. In the coronation procession of 1901 no one seems to have seen any *lèse-majesté* in the fact that the king and queen were impersonated by Gervase and his sister Margaret. There is a record of an old folks' supper provided by Benson and his wife, at which forty-one guests were given a 'first class repast' with members of the family providing entertainment. The supper was for some years a frequent, probably an annual, event. Benson had married Elizabeth Storrs Walker in 1872. She was a fine character and a great help to him, she died in 1904. They had three daughters and two sons.

Benson was an active supporter of the causes of temperance and of Liberalism, and so were his children. His daughters, especially Margaret, frequently spoke at public meetings in Bentham and surrounding villages for these causes. And it may be noted that these children had, in Benson's sister, Isabella O. Ford of Leeds, an aunt who was a prominent national figure in the movement for women's suffrage.

A good picture of Benson and his family is given by Roger Clark in a letter describing a visit in 1892 (*Quaker Inheritance 1871-1961. A portrait of Roger Clark of Street*, by Percy Lovell, 1970, p. 72). After telling how Benson met him at High Bentham station and drove him in an Irish jaunting car 'cheerfully behind a spanking grey cob' to Brook Cottage, Roger Clark continues 'the house is extremely snug ... We were warmly welcomed and to come from ... Leeds into such beautiful country and such a kindly welcome from an enthusiastic, warm hearted and amusing family, was a change truly worth a great deal. Benson has all the excessive kindness and broadness of Rawlinson [his brother, of Yealand, founder of Ford & Warren, Solicitors, Leeds] and is equally well informed. But in addition he is so tremendously enthusiastic and lively and entertaining that really he is altogether a man after my own heart ... and their way of living is simpler, more natural and countrified. On Saturday we went over the mill and played hockey with the boys in the morning and after dinner went a

splendid walk to an ancestral farm of Benson's right away up
on the moors [Mewith Head Hall] . . . Benson is an ideal land-
lord. I know he spends far more on improvements than he
gets in rents.' But Benson could sometimes be rather irascible.
Naturally he could not always avoid village disputes and he
was involved in a long-standing feud with the rector apparently
over the use of the schoolroom. The rights of the case are not
known but we can be sure that they were not all on Benson's
side.

Benson was joined in the business by his elder son, Charles.
Born in 1879, Charles went to Leighton Park School and
started work in the mill in 1897. He left for the three years
1899–1902 to take a degree in engineering at Clare College,
Cambridge where he was captain and stroke of the College boat
and in trials for the University eight. In 1902 he returned to the
mill in which he gave unbroken service until three weeks
before his death in January 1964. About 1905 he became joint
manager with his father, and since the latter, from that time
until 1918, was giving more and more time to public and
Quaker service, Charles took the main responsibility, although
in 1907 Harold Metford Warner joined the firm and took over
the management of the machinery. After serving his apprenticeship in engineering Harold Warner had worked as an engineer
with Canadian railways. His brother Reginald, after similar
training, entered another side of the silk trade, founding the
Gainsborough Silk Weaving Co. in Sudbury, Suffolk, which
for many years was a customer of Ford, Ayrton. Harold
Warner was a great asset to the business and his death in 1913
was a severe loss. Edward Ayrton, another kindly, much loved
man, took care of the secretarial and accountancy side and his
work was a model of exactness. After thirty-eight years invaluable service, first as partner and then as director, he died in
1926. Other senior members of the firm will be mentioned
later, but the main control of the mill from 1918, and even for
some years before that, until January 1964, was the responsibility of Charles Ford. He had married in 1909, Margaret

Harvey, daughter of the William Harvey of Leeds who had been an original partner in the firm from 1870 to 1877. She died in 1917 leaving one daughter, Elizabeth Rawlinson, who married J. H. P. Pafford in 1941. In 1919 Charles married Helen B. Byles who died in 1969. They had no children, but Helen Ford, herself active in public service, fully shared her husband's interests and was a great help to him in discussing problems connected with any of these and not least those of the mill. Other members of the Ford family were connected with the mill, notably Gervase Lawson Ford, younger brother to Charles.

Like his father and brother, Charles was an able man of absolute integrity. He too saw the mill as a trust and regarded everyone who worked in it as a colleague and friend. There was nothing purely sentimental about this. It was Charles Ford's attitude to life. At the Quaker memorial meeting after his death, William Bruce, one of his oldest friends and a former overlooker and Employee Director at the mill, said words to the effect 'Of Faith, Hope and Charity we are told that the greatest is Charity. It may be so, but Faith is great. It was because we knew that Charles Ford had faith in us that we had faith in ourselves, in each other and above all in him. There was confidence and no suspicion, and that was why all he did at the mill was a success.' When the firm changed to a 40-hour week Charles is quoted in the *Lancaster Guardian*, 5 August 1960, as saying that Ford, Ayrton 'is not a money-making affair. It never has been. It goes something beyond that. We aim that it should be a concern which shall create happiness and trust of each other.'

Benson was a fair-minded but strict disciplinarian. Charles, a gentle, kindly man who brought his Christian Quaker principles fully into his daily life, obtained at least as good a response from everyone in the mill by a rather different approach. There was never a strike, and although of course there were occasional differences of opinion on the way things should be done, and even on policy, and some inevitable clashes of personalities, there was little serious friction and never anything that could be called an industrial dispute in the whole history of the mill. Charles also did his share of public and Quaker service. He supported the Labour movement and was in 1921 invited to stand as Labour parliamentary candidate for the Skipton constituency, and in 1923 and 1927 for Lancaster, but he had no wish to become a politician and nothing would have made him desert his responsibility at the mill. Yet he gave much public service; he was active as a magistrate from 1932, Commissioner of Income Tax from 1918, governor of Bentham Grammar School from 1921 to 1963 and for many years its chairman, member and chairman of the Settle Divisional Executive of the Education Committee, chairman of the Bentham Parish Council and of the Bentham Gas Company and other bodies. In industry he had been chairman of the British Silk Spinners Association and of the Joint Industrial Council for Silk and member for some time of the Silk Club which met in Manchester from 1885 to 1959. His Quaker service included three years as Assistant and forty-six years as Clerk of Bentham Preparative Meeting, five years Clerk of Settle Monthly Meeting and for terms of three years Assistant Clerk, then Clerk, of Yorkshire Quarterly Meeting. He also gave long service on the Brighouse, Leeds and Settle Trust Funds Committee, the Quarterly Meeting Nominations Committee and the Yorkshire Friends Service Committee. Perhaps Charles held some of his appointments rather too long: if so it is a fault not uncommon in many who give dedicated service.

He was a keen supporter of many causes, particularly those of peace and the welfare of all distressed peoples and of animals, and of many local activities in Bentham. Yorkshire, and Yorkshire dialect stories, which he loved to tell, and cricket, especially and naturally Yorkshire cricket, were consuming interests, and the second of his two main hobbies was photography. The first was railways. As a trained engineer he had an almost professional knowledge of the technical side of everything to do with railways and he was also interested in railway administration. It would be untrue to say that Bradshaw was his favourite reading, but it always gave him much pleasure to be asked advice on the best way of making a cross-country journey by rail; and he greatly enjoyed the railway journeys in travelling for his firm. Vegetarian, abstainer and — except for a very short period — non-smoker, his own wants were simple. He never owned a car, but he loved the open air and used his bicycle until he was over eighty. He had a large collection of books on railways which he presented in 1963, with books on Quakerism, to the Library of the newly formed University of Lancaster, where they formed the beginnings of important special collections in these two subjects.

Over and over again come testimonies to Charles Ford's fine character, not only from those who knew him well, but from strangers. So a working man, who, after a talk by Charles at Saltaire Adult School in 1926 on Co-Partnership, had felt on reaching home that his attitude and questions to the speaker might have seemed hostile. He wrote to say that this was not so but that even more 'I felt your worthy personality and spirit was a feast, your frankness, your sense of absolute justice, and perhaps above all your sincerity, well you came near a veritable "Child of God" . . . and I want you to accept my very cordial thanks for . . . the privilege of having come in contact with such a noble soul'. A Bootham sixth-form boy in an undated letter wrote the day after Charles had given an address at the school: 'I have heard many speakers . . . but can truthfully say that to hear you last night was the greatest pleasure of all. Few indeed are the people who can bring their message to the hearts of their listeners in the way you did.' Charles did indeed speak to the heart as well as the head. Even press reporters — often held to be a hard-bitten race — had the same reaction, as is shown in *The Times* report in 1926 quoted below (p. 15). But there was nothing naïve in his love for his fellows. Unwilling to see humbug, laziness or any unworthiness in others, he was yet a good judge of character. He was aware of these things and on rare occasions rebuked them, but his normal method was to continue to trust, love and help others in spite of their failings; and in so doing he often did indeed help. An active, happy, unselfish and lovable man, *The Craven Herald* of 17 January 1964, in its obituary notice, said, 'He was wise, sympathetic and kind and therefore a man to whom others naturally brought their troubles, and the number he helped by his advice, and often in more practical ways, can never be known . . . the most companionable of men . . . he was happy, and he was the constant cause of happiness in others'. On leaving an annual mill meeting, at which Charles always presided, an employee was overheard to say, 'I would follow that man anywhere'; and the head of another firm in the trade, in one of the first letters received after Charles Ford's death, wrote 'With Mr. Ford passes away the best loved and most respected man in the trade'. Comments of this kind could be multiplied, but in those two, from within and outside the mill, perhaps everything is said.

Economists are divided in diagnosing causes of inflation and industrial troubles. Some think that these things are mainly economic and stem from world market forces, while others believe that they arise chiefly from social conflict between workers and owners of capital, and that as long as workers are interested only in wages and not in the use of capital, and owners are interested only in the latter and the profits it can make, there can be no solution. This grossly over-simplifies a highly complex problem which could not be pursued here even if the writers were competent to do so. It is mentioned because the Fords' determination to ensure that workers and owners shared interest in the work, in the management and in the use of capital and its rewards — in what is now called worker participation, in the fullest sense — was not because this might obviate industrial troubles or improve output or make people happy, but simply because it was humanly the right and therefore the only thing to do. And so Charles, with his father's approval, and with warm support from Gervase and other members of the family, started in 1917 to pay a bonus from

profits to all the 200 employees. In 1919 a definite scheme was
launched for continuing this bonus to workers, and also to
shareholders on their interest only; and dividends, to vary with
profits, were to have a maximum of 6 per cent. At the same time
workers were invited to become shareholders, and these were
entitled to elect two of their fellows as employee Directors of
the firm. Workers who were shareholders of course received
their bonus as workers as well as that on the interest on their
shares. A sickness and hardship benefit fund for employees
was established by allocations from the Company's profits;
weekly hours were cut from 55½ to 44 (and in 1960 to 40)
the mill being closed on Saturdays. In 1929 were started a
Thrift Fund and a Pension Fund which was entirely non-
contributory, being built up from the firm's profits. Pensions
were paid to employees who retired at sixty or over with at
least twenty years' service; and on a pensioner's death his
widow received the pension for five more years. Since 1926
employees were entitled to holidays with pay, the entitlement
being originally one week plus the statutory holidays and
latterly nineteen working days in all. During holidays piece-
workers were paid the day rates.

The profit-sharing introduced in 1917 and the co-partnership
and profit-sharing plan of 1919 were approved by the founder
but planned and carried out by Charles. He was strongly supported by other members of the family even though it meant
loss of income to them. Charles received notable assistance from
his brother Gervase, a prominent Leeds solicitor, head of the
family firm of Ford & Warren, who was a Director of Ford,
Ayrton from 1919 until his death in 1963. He too was deeply
interested in anything for the good of the workers, and for
forty-four years gave — entirely without fee of any kind —
the benefit of his wide business experience, professional legal
knowledge and wise counsel. With the exception of one case
where a small fee was paid for four years, all the family Directors
who were not employed at the mill always served without fee
or any payment beyond travelling expenses.

Yet the success of these measures, and particularly the co-partnership and profit-sharing, was not simply due to their intrinsic value, but to the spirit in which they were promoted and carried out. In reporting the Leeds conference, organized by the Labour Co-partnership Association, of 18 September 1926, *The Times* of 20 September gave prominence to Charles Ford's account of Ford, Ayrton and added 'The conference was greatly impressed, not only with the liberality of this scheme, but with the personality displayed by its founder'. Charles himself said (*News Chronicle*, 25.IX.26) 'What . . . are the motives of co-partnership? Is it an attempt to pacify labour, or does it spring from a conviction that every worker has an inherent right to take a greater share in the product he produces than mere wage? If the latter is the motive, then the foundations are laid for real peace and good-will . . . Much is heard about good-will in industry — as if it could be called upon at a moment's notice . . . Good-will is the result of a life's work, and it rests upon confidence. Confidence will follow upon co-partnership and profit-sharing, if they are founded upon a right motive'. Charles saw the workers as his partners, and their rights, their interest and welfare, as well as their participation in the business, were his constant concern. He set out his views, which included a strong belief in Trade Unionism, in several places, for example, in his article on 'Profit-sharing' in *Pitman's Dictionary* (Book List 33), and 'Harmony in Industry' (*The Friend*, 30 January 1942, 35–6, Book List 32) where he expressed his belief that a small business can produce as cheaply and efficiently as a large one.

With men of such fine character, having such principles in their lives and work, it is not surprising that there were no industrial disputes at Ford, Ayrton in the 100 years of its history. We have said that the mill now and then had conflicting personalities, and say it again simply to ensure that no one should think that life in the mill was that of some unreal Arcadia. It was nothing of the kind: it was healthy, robust mill life. It is a truism that wherever people are grouped for any activity it is almost certain that at times there will be some degree of conflict; and Ford, Ayrton was no exception. But the constant, dominant keynote of the mill and the spirit running deeply through it was one of harmony. In 1966 Will Hawkins could truly say 'At the present day, the working partnership which Charles Ford helped to mould persists in an atmosphere of friendliness and cordiality which so often is missing in the huge industrial combines of the modern age' (Book List 27).

Man-made fibres were responsible for considerable falling off in the silk trade generally, but the immediate reason for the closure of the last silk-spinning mill in Britain was competition from Chinese and Italian spinners. These, with modern buildings and plant, lower wages, longer working hours, easier and cheaper access to raw materials, were able, in spite of import duties, to undersell in Britain all British silk spinners, including Ford, Ayrton, and heavily to undersell them in the rest of the world. Ford, Ayrton held out longer than the others, but even with today's hindsight, no reorganization of the firm with resources available could have continued to meet this competition from overseas, particularly as no funds were available for essential modernization of buildings and plant. It was inevitable, but sad indeed, that for these reasons the country had to lose a firm which, although small, could truly claim to have been a model of successful co-operation between workers and management.

3

The Place and more of the People

THERE ARE in fact two places, for the firm spent the first seven years of its life in Leeds before moving to Low Bentham, also in Yorkshire. In Leeds the small mill took its place easily, but hardly noticed, a drop in the ocean of a great industrial city, where it can have made little impact even on the community of its immediate neighbourhood. Established in 1870, productive work began on Monday, 3 January 1871 with four employees which increased to ten by the end of the week. Staff numbers varied, but in 1877 there were fifty-six, nearly all women and girls. But even in the opening week there was one man, Mr A. Stead, and in 1877 Edward Wilkinson was works manager and he, with his brother John, moved to Bentham with the firm. Ned Wilkinson, a hard and accurate worker and a good disciplinarian, left in 1906. About 1877 two silk dressers from a mill near Harrogate, John Lockwood and George Marshall, also came to Bentham.

As used in this book the name Bentham or 'the village' normally refers to Low Bentham, since that is where the Ford, Ayrton mill was and is; with postal address Low Mills, Bentham, via Lancaster. The township — in Yorkshire but on the Lancashire border — actually consists of two villages, Low and High Bentham, about a mile apart. Of these Low is the older and contains the parish church, and High is the larger. They became separate ecclesiastical parishes in 1837. Bentham, spelt Benetain, Benetham, is mentioned in Domesday Book, 1086, and, according to the English Place-Name Society, means 'Homestead amongst the bent-grass'. Populations in

17

1877 were about 800 (Low) and 1,400 (High) and in 1970 about 850 and 1,750.

Bentham was chosen no doubt because a mill building of about the right size was available, there was room for expansion and a labour force; road and rail communications were good and there was not only water power and clean air but a plentiful supply of good soft water so essential for the discharging of raw silk waste. There had been another silk-spinning mill at Wray, some three miles west of Bentham which had a long but broken history and may even have been working in 1877 although it closed soon after. Benson Ford had bought dressed silk from Wray when he was at Leeds. Pauline H. S. McCann in 'A Comparative study of Halton and Wray' (unpublished M.A. thesis at the University of Lancaster) notes that there was a silk mill in Wray from 1829–34 and that 'The waters of the Roeburn are supposed to be particularly suited for the boiling of silk'. Ford, Ayrton employed some silk dressers from Wray and the firm had a spinning frame, known as the Wray frame, which had been bought from the Wray mill.

The Low Bentham mill had been the weaving department of the High Bentham Flax Spinning Mill, and dates on a stone in the west wall record building (probably original) in 1785, destruction by fire in 1852 and rebuilding the same year. In 1928 the upper floor was rebuilt and extended. The water-wheel 'Lily of the Wenning', 24 ft. by 12 ft. by 12 ft., maximum 50 h.p. was part of the old mill. It had been installed about 1821 and continued to give service until 1921. An original source of power was the river Wenning from which a cut had been made which drove the old water-wheel until that was removed in 1921 and two water turbines installed made by Gilbert Gilkes and Co. of Kendal which were in use until the mill closed. There was also an old steam beam engine which was replaced in 1886 by an inverted vertical 160 h.p. steam engine built by Hick, Hargreaves of Bolton at the cost, including installation, of £680. Affectionately known as 'Lizzie', this remarkable engine was in perfect order when the mill closed. The mill took great pride in Lizzie which was looked after by a series of devoted and skilled engine-men. Up to December 1889 names are not known, but from then on they were T. Tomlinson, 1889–91; J. Gregory, 1891–2; R. Bibby, 1892–4; C. Lodge, 1894–1935; J. Fletcher, 1936; A. E. Wilcock, 1937–54; W. Noble, 1954–62; E. Murray, 1963–70.

The engine was assisted by the turbines by a rope drive from the turbine shaft to the main shaft driven by the engine. One turbine generated 50 h.p. and one 30 h.p. They were arranged so that both operated together when water was plentiful, but as the supply diminished the 50 h.p. turbine ran on its own taking all available water, and when the water dropped still further, the 30 h.p. turbine ran on its own, thus ensuring that maximum power was obtained from the amount of water available in the driest of summers.

The firm made constant efforts to keep the mill and its plant up to date and in good condition, and from the mid 1920's, when such things are first mentioned, the Minutes of almost every Board meeting record major or minor repairs, improvements or additions. The Circular Dressing Machines added in the 1930's are mentioned on p. 38; four new Dandy Rovers were bought in 1949; the two weirs were repaired in 1956 at a cost of nearly £2,000; in 1959 the makers gave the engine a complete overhaul (£2,000) and in 1961 two Bigwood Underfeed Stokers were installed (£2,000) and the mill yard completely resurfaced (£2,000); an Alternator was installed in 1964 and a Savio hank to cone Winding machine (£1,600 less £400 Government grant) in 1966. A good deal of second-hand machinery was bought from other Silk Spinners when they closed: even as late as September 1968 £1,350 was spent — perhaps unwisely — in this way.

In 1900, when Ford, Ayrton was registered as a limited liability company, Benson Ford leased the mill and its lands and other property which he owned in Bentham, to the company. In 1914 he set up another company called Brook Cottage Land Co. Ltd to which he transferred his ownership of all lands and properties he had leased to Ford, Ayrton. Hence from 1914 to its closure, Ford, Ayrton rented its land and buildings from Brook Cottage Land Co., which later became a Trust. The Trustees were always members of the Ford family. It was wound up in 1970 when Ford, Ayrton closed. The firm paid for the new Winding room built in 1928 and in payment for it Brook Cottage Land Co. gave the firm fifteen cottages in Bentham which were occupied by employees or pensioners and later sold to the occupants.

'*Bonnie Bentham* as the villagers delight to call the picturesque old place' (H. Speight: *The Craven and N.W. Yorkshire highlands*, 1892, p. 200) is indeed a pretty village in a setting of considerable natural beauty. On the river Wenning which joins the Lune about six miles to the west, near Hornby, it is in a shallow, fertile valley with high fells and moorlands to the north, east, and south. Within a mile or two these rise steeply, as to the Big Stone on Burn Moor (1,200 ft.) to the south, and to the northeast Ingleborough (2,373 ft.) with Pen-y-ghent and Whernside — the famous three peaks, all of which those who would qualify as fell walkers must climb in one and the same day. The whole countryside, although it can be bleak in winter, is full of lovely becks and dales, delightful for walking and picnicking. The nearest towns are Kirkby Lonsdale (10 m.), Settle (12 m.), and Lancaster (15 m.) and the sea is only 13 miles away, beyond Carnforth.

The re-opening of Low Mills by Benson Ford & Co. was vitally important to the village, and the mill retained that importance to its close. The coming of the Ford family also meant something to the village, and it can fairly be said that they and many others associated with the mill exercised a lasting influence on Bentham.

In the mill itself there was considerable expansion in processes and numbers. At Leeds there was no dressing department, and silk was bought already dressed. But at Bentham a dressing room was immediately set up and the whole processing of raw silk through to the finished yarn was carried out in the mill, with the exception of dyeing, a specialist process which the mill never undertook. This completion of the production line involved, among other things, making gas, not only for lighting but for the gassing room. Gas was available in Leeds but not then in Bentham, and so gas plant and holder were set up and used until 1955 when gas was laid on from the North Western Gas grid. There were many extensions and alterations to the buildings: for instance, in 1896 a room was rented in a disused cotton mill at Burton-in-Lonsdale, 2½ miles away. The reeling, knifing, winding and copping were transferred there, in charge of Adam Wallbank, a Burton man, who incidentally was one of the Employee Directors first appointed in 1924 after co-partnership had been started in 1919. A horse and cart were used to carry the yarn to and from Burton. But all this proved uneconomical and after a year or two the Burton department was closed and a new room was built over the raw silk warehouse (later the dining room) and all processing was carried out in the mill. Adam was an extremely loyal, capable and industrious overlooker, who lived for his work. He often worked at Burton long after hours without any thought of booking overtime, and he established a tradition of fine work in the winding room. The hard-worked horse, 'Tommy', was also used to take goods to the station or post and to fetch coal from the station, and sometimes, with the Ford jaunting car, for mill personnel or visitors, chiefly to and from the station.

For a short time Benson Ford owned one of the first cars in Bentham, an Aroll Johnson. It was driven by James James, who had been the Ford's coachman and who also continued to drive the horse and cart and jaunting car. In the mill and village he was known as 'Jimjams', which he accepted, although he would sometimes good-naturedly complain 'I've only got one name for both my names and darned if I can be called by it for either'. He was succeeded by Jack Berry.

Although most of the employees lived in Low Bentham, some came from High and some from surrounding districts including Burton-in-Lonsdale, and all walked: there were no buses in the early days and even bicycles came later. There was a higher proportion of men and boys than there had been at Leeds, and only men were overlookers; but most of the staff were women and girls. Older members of the mill, like William Bruce and Charles Ford, were sometimes heard to comment on the startling difference in the appearance of the women from the point of view of clothing in the early days, particularly before 1918, as compared with the post-1945 period. Formerly they wore clogs and dull coloured shawls over their heads — traditional garb of the mill girl — and of course long skirts which were always dark coloured; and all this presented a drab, uniform appearance which, as can easily be imagined, was in marked contrast to the bright, neat, fashionable clothing of the women and girls of the later period.

One interesting source of women-power was a Liverpool orphanage for girls. From 1890 or earlier until about 1910 girls of fifteen upwards were obtained from an orphanage in Liverpool and boarded in one of the mill cottages (No. 6, now occupied by William Bruce) under the care of a woman supervisor. For the week ending 8 January 1890 the wage book records that 'gratuities' were paid to twelve orphans ranging from 3d. to 2/- each and that Miss Sedgwick is 'paid up to Friday night for the orphans'. Later there were two supervisors, the Misses Fortescue, sisters. Twelve seems to have been a maximum number and all reports and personal recollections speak extremely well of these girls. Indeed Will Bruce, with a twinkle in his eye, says 'Aye, they were some gay lasses', adding that they were good workers too. Many had Irish names, and not only were they a fresh, interesting element in the mill and life of the village, but they had an enterprising community spirit of their own and gave or took part in village concerts. The *Lancaster Standard*, 27 December 1895, describes a public 'Concert by Orphans' in the mill dining room. The girls had been 'under the tuition of Mr. Boyd for music and for dialogue under Miss M. Ford' — always known as Miss

PLATE IIIA. Some employees who retired in 1935 showing length of service in years. (Left to right): Thomas Robinson 55; Henry R. Nutter 49; John W. Lister 56; John Parker 58; John Adamthwaite 52. Average service 54 years

PLATE IIIB. Directors and Company Secretary, 1939.
Standing (left to right): Herbert Ramskill, Thomas Bownass (Secretary). Seated: William Bruce, Gervase Ford, Charles Ford, Robert Forrester

PLATE IV. William Bruce (on left) in 1970, aged 90; with Ford, Ayrton 57 years. William Hawkins, with Ford, Ayrton 24 years, Managing Director, 1964–70. Reproduced by courtesy of *The Lancaster Guardian*

Margaret in mill and village. The dialogue, a comic number by Misses Corcoran and McCassellan, was apparently the hit of the evening. Apart from all this, one or two of the girls married local men, and some of the descendants worked in the mill. Altogether the introduction of the orphans seems to have been an unqualified success. They made a happy impact on mill and village. Their employment was a good thing for the girls as it gave them a start in life in good employment and good for the mill in introducing useful labour when it was needed. In using this source of labour Ford, Ayrton were, of course, following a fairly common practice in industry. Girls were not taken from the orphanage when employees could be had locally.

Although most of the employees have been women, the mill has always had a number of men: many of these were very able, some memorable for their quality, and a few, of course, were 'characters'. An attempt to list some of the men had to be abandoned for it was impossible now even to find the names of all who should be included, and there was no wish to give offence by unfair omissions. Tom Bownass, whose notes are full of warm human touches — has mentioned many men and women, who, as he generously puts it, 'have helped me by their example' and made his long service at the mill very happy; but he himself advises against an attempt to list names. Yet a few of his comments, which throw light on personalities in a few words, should not be omitted. He never mentions those of poor quality, of which, of course, the mill had its share. Of John Hodgson, yarn warehouseman, he simply says 'nothing shoddy passed John'. Charlie Jackson, dressing room overlooker, invariably used the phrase 'worked just fair' in his written report on every batch. If there were enquiries he would repeat these words, but he had a range of inflexion and emphasis in his voice which was understood and which gave accurate information. Jack Adamthwaite did a job generally thought of as dull, namely, looking after the spindle bands, mending or renewing them as required in order to keep every spindle running. But this job mattered and Charles Ford had a knack of appreciating and showing everyone that they and their work mattered. Jack was a conscientious, quiet man much respected for his devotion to duty. The old, frayed and oily bands were no further use in the mill but were handy for gardeners to tie up beans, etc. Tom once asked Jack if he could have a few for garden use, and Jack's slow, careful reply was 'I cannot give you any, Thomas (he never abbreviated names), but I'll show you where they are'.

Since the women did not obtain senior posts their names are not so well known; but everyone agreed that the women were the backbone of the work force in the mill, many coming to work in snow and other bad weather, with just as much determination as the men, and doing hard and often tedious jobs devotedly, cheerfully and with skill. There were many families with long tradition of excellent service to the mill, as for example the Wilcock family. Here there were at least a father, with two sons, Alec an overlooker, Albert, engine-man, and both of them Employee Directors. Albert's two daughters and one son, Colin, an overlooker, all worked in the mill as did seven daughters of another brother of Alec and Albert, who himself did not work in the mill. To complete this family picture, there were at least nine great-grandchildren of the first mentioned father employed in the mill at various times — making at least twenty-two in all. Will Bruce was the third of five generations in the mill and one of his grand-daughters was employed there when the mill closed. There were many other families and many individual persons with over 40 and some with over 50 years' service.

The only concern about mentioning even these names is because there is no space for many others, equally worthy of mention. Miss Isobel (Bella) Carter, 6 Victoria Cottages, Bentham, started at the mill in about 1896, aged fourteen and left in 1946. In conversation in 1973 she has vivid memories of the mill. She well remembered Benson Ford as 'a father figure who knew everyone personally. He took us into his confidence and told us details when trade was bad and kept us on cleaning windows, walls, floors, etc. We had such a happy time at the mill. It was a second home.' Were there space, there is no doubt at all that many reminiscences like this could still be obtained. But mention must now be made of other senior members of the staff.

In 1913 Fred Crossley, of Bolton, joined the firm as mill manager in succession to Harold Warner, and in 1924 was nominated by the Directors as an Employee Director. A gifted engineer, he left in 1933. Thomas Bownass, who had joined the firm in 1905, was Secretary from 1925 until his retirement in 1954 after a few months short of fifty years' service. An able and devoted member of the staff he was, and is, a most interesting and many-sided man, skilled in various handicrafts including hand-loom weaving, an amateur artist and writer of occasional poetry. Mention has already been made of his invaluable contribution to this booklet. He was also the originator and editor of Ford, Ayrton's pamphlets 'Spun Silk Yarns'. In addition to Adam Wallbank, the other Employee Director elected in 1924 by his fellows was William Bruce. He joined the firm in 1889 aged ten and was for many years overlooker in the Preparing room before he retired in 1946 after fifty-seven years' service. In his early years a preacher in local Methodist chapels, he gave other public service, being Chairman of the village Old Age Pensioners society, trustee of the village hall, and on other committees and a strong supporter of the Labour Party. He was also a keen fisherman, a robust character full of good humour and common sense. In 1969 Dr L. Dowell made a tape recording of reminiscences of the mill by Will Bruce which is a most interesting record.

In 1929 Robert Forrester entered the mill as deputy to Charles Ford, becoming a Director in 1931. He died in 1959. He was perhaps the most intellectually able man the mill ever had. He had a degree in science and was a skilled mathematician. He foresaw the menace of foreign competition and was an early advocate of electrification and modernization of the whole mill. It is impossible now to estimate what might have happened if his views had been shared by Charles Ford and the other Directors who had a more conservative attitude to mill development. The life of the mill might have been shortened if the expense of modernization had not given ability to produce cheaper yarn, or lengthened if that had been achieved. But there is probably little in it either way, for even if modernization had been successful it is hard to believe that the degree of success could have been enough to defeat foreign competition. In addition to his intellectual brilliance Robert Forrester was a man of great personal charm, dedicated to the service of the mill.

In 1947 William Hawkins joined the firm. Nominated an Employee Director in October 1949 and made a Permanent Director in February 1956 he succeeded Tom Bownass as Secretary in 1954 and in 1959 also took over Robert Forrester's duties as Manager. On the death of Charles Ford in 1964 he became Managing Director, and was succeeded as Secretary by Joan Parker (now Mrs N. Brewster) who had been secretary to Charles Ford. Will Hawkins thus held key posts, and latterly the chief responsibility in the mill, during times of relative prosperity and throughout the period of its final decline; and it fell to him to organize and largely to carry out the sad, heavy and complicated task of running the mill down and finally bringing about its closure. And this, with decreasing staff and in spite of many difficulties and frustrations, he well and truly did — with able help in the last weeks from his wife, Mrs Norah Hawkins. He was the last to leave the ship which he had served so well from the time he joined it. Few people who have not been involved in the closing of a business can appreciate the strain of the professional and personal worries which such an operation is bound to cause. It is good to have an opportunity of paying testimony to the excellent way in which Will Hawkins carried through a most difficult and exhausting task.

An important appointment in the last years of the mill was that of Frank L. Ford, great-grandson of the founder, grandson of Gervase and elder son of Ursula. Frank had taken a degree in forestry at University College, Bangor and joined the mill as a trainee in 1964. He went through every department and, becoming virtually assistant Managing Director, joined the Board in 1966. But his keenness, ability and energy could not change what had by then become inevitable.

In 1959, Ursula O. Ford, daughter of Gervase, and in 1963 Elizabeth R. Pafford, daughter of Charles, and her husband John Pafford, joined the Board and all remained Directors until the mill closed.

4

The raw material, processing, history and uses

THIS IS NOT the place for a history and description of sericulture and the manufacture of silk yarn and its uses. The intention here is little more than to give a general idea of what is done, and not to attempt detailed explanation of technical matters. This is not a book for the expert: he will know, and probably all others will readily guess, that the following account is only a brief and simplified outline of parts of a long, complicated and fascinating story, of which fuller details can be obtained from works in the Book List on pp. 69–73. Readers will also be aware of the dangers of over-simplification and will know that occasionally some loss of accuracy may result because full details cannot be given. It is hoped that if this does occur it is never of major importance. Technical processes are rarely easy to describe, especially without diagrams, and the writers were comforted to receive from a former employee of nearly fifty years' service, a description of the dressing room with a covering note which read, 'I found it very difficult to describe the dressing process in a way that would be understandable by a lay person. I've read it through and don't understand it myself!'

The silk-worm in developing into its chrysalis state, encases itself in a cocoon of fine silk filament or thread and this material is the raw silk. The getting of this may be divided into two separate fields of operation of which the first is called that of *nett silk* and the second that of *waste silk*. Both these materials are the same raw silk, but there is a difference which will soon become clear. It may be said without more delay that silk spinning, which was Ford, Ayrton's business, used only waste silk. (In parenthesis it may be noted that Ford, Ayrton did occasionally spin a little man-made fibre, but its basic raw material was always waste silk.)

Most of the silk-worms are killed in the cocoon, by heat or chemical treatment which does not injure the cocoon. The cocoons are then softened in hot water until it is possible to pick up the fine filament on the cocoon and to unwind it in an unbroken length, and the length reeled from a good cocoon averages about 1,100 yards (Gaddum). A number of cocoons, anything from four to twelve, are unwound together: the filaments are brought into contact and the softened gum on them solidifies and so makes one thread. This is wound or reeled on to bobbins and is used by silk throwsters who produce from it silk yarn known as nett silk.

But, as will easily be imagined, all through these processes there will be 'waste'. Sources of this waste could be arranged in three main groups:

1. From cocoons before they are in any way processed. There is usually some fluffy silk around the twig to which the cocoon is attached. Next, in order to propagate the species, some silkworms must be allowed to live. Each of these — now changed into a moth — emits a substance which dissolves an end of the coccoon, making a large hole permitting the moth to emerge but breaking the filaments and so leaving the silk on these pierced cocoons unfit for reeling. Some cocoons are deformed or damaged and sometimes two are stuck together and silk cannot be reeled. All this silk is 'waste' for the spinner.

2. Waste from reeling; filature or steam waste. Before the unbroken thread can be reached, an outer layer of silk has to be stripped from the cocoon. There is also an inner layer of unreelable silk on the cocoon, and some cocoons for various reasons refuse to reel, all yielding waste. All this is known as knubbs or frisons and 'provides the bulk of all waste silk

brought by spinners' (Gaddum): for every 100 lb. of reeled silk there may be 20 to 30 lb. of knubbs.

3. Waste from throwing or weaving processes, known as gum or thread waste. Ends break in reeling and re-reeling and pieces of waste filament result. This is sometimes referred to as the best waste for the spinner, but Ford, Ayrton woud have had reservations on this. In the first place ordinary gum waste often had too much twist and was found unsuitable for spinning. The gum waste called tram had very little twist and was good. But as the throwing and weaving firms came to use more and more man-made fibres some of these and other impurities would get mixed with the tram which therefore needed much cleaning. When this had been done Ford, Ayrton used to find that the best waste, giving the finest lustre, was made by blending one-sixth to one-third cleaned tram with frisons.

It will thus be seen that the essential difference between raw nett and raw waste silk is that the former is an unbroken long thread of silk and the latter a tangled mass of short pieces of different lengths. This waste silk, which accounts for about half the total silk produced by the silkworm, is obtained chiefly from China and Russia, from Turkey, Greece and Bulgaria, and some other places in the Middle East, and from Italy. Waste obtained from India was of poor quality. Japan produces more silk than any other country but uses practically all of it herself. From about 1955 China supplied very little waste, but sold silk already dressed. Raw waste silk comes in many varieties and qualities depending on its source and how it has been obtained. The only known commercial production of silk cocoons in this country is at the Lullingstone Silk Farm owned by Zoë, Lady Hart Dyke, at Ayot St Lawrence, Herts. Nett silk is reeled here but resultant waste is small in quantity.

In the early days Ford, Ayrton bought a lot of steam waste and the well-known waste called China Curlies. Waste was bought through several agents, but particularly from H. T.

Gaddum & Co. who were in Manchester until they moved to Macclesfield about 1965. Benson and then Charles Ford used to go frequently to Manchester to see samples of waste at various agents. From 1948 the firm bought frisons and tram gum waste, and a good waste called Kikai Kibizzo or Japan Curlies, and Canton steam waste and Shanghai knubbs. Several agents were used including R. Desco, London, various merchants in Italy, including Oswaldo Helbring, but particularly H. T. Gaddum. Prices fluctuated widely: before 1939 steam waste was normally 1/6d. to 2/- a lb., but at least once went as low as 8½d.

Waste silk arrives at the spinning mill packed in bales and is, at this stage, a rather hard, unattractive material of a dirty yellow or greyish colour.

The processing line at Ford, Ayrton was divided into eight main departments: 1. Raw Warehouse and Silk Discharging; 2. Dressing; 3. Preparing; 4. Spinning; 5. Twisting; 6. Gassing; 7. Winding; 8. Yarn Warehouse. It will be convenient to refer briefly to these processes in the present tense. On receipt in department 1, the first operation, after checking and weighing, is to boil the raw material in water — with a little soda ash if the silk is greasy — to discharge the natural gum, dirt and other impurities in the silk: the gum, known as sericin — for which it is surprising that no commercial use has been found — may account for anything between 25 and 35 per cent of the weight of the raw silk, which, incidentally, is therefore a weight on which freight has been wastefully paid. After the cleaned, discharged silk has first been dried and then allowed in a natural way to absorb a little moisture and so regain its natural condition, it acquires something of the beauty, the softness and lustre always associated with silk: but it is still tangled. The Lancashire spinner's boast, 'I can spin anything with two ends' states the main requirement for his art. Material for spinning must not be in a tangle but in lengths; and department 2, Dressing, sets out to transform a tangle into lengths. This is commonly regarded as the most important and perhaps the most difficult operation in the series. By the first process, known as 'filling' the silk is straightened out and cut into slabs about 7 in. long. Each slab will, of course, contain many pieces shorter than this. By a combing process the silk is then opened and drawn out into lengths or drafts and all the fibres are parallelized by the combing: drafts of the longest filaments are called 1st, the next longest 2nd, and so on. The drafts of dressed silk are placed on sheets of frosted glass under which strong lights show up any foreign materials or small tangles which are picked out by hand.

The silk is then passed to 3, the Preparing room, where it goes through a series of operations of which the first is spreading. In this it is spread on a travelling sheet and carried to a roller of a certain circumference. When the operative thinks that the roller contains three ounces she strips the roller by winding the silk round her hand and so makes what is called a lap. Here is the foundation of the count system — a lap of a certain length weighing three ounces. The other operations in this room are drawing, roving and dandy-roving which consist of further straightening and drawing out so that the laps become progressively thinner and longer until they look like untwisted thin ropes of silk. These are known, in their first state, as slivers, in which there is no twist, and then as rovings, in which there is just enough twist to hold the rovings together when mounted for spinning, an operation for which the silk is now ready.

Spinning is carried out in the next department 4, by 'ring spinning' processes similar to those employed for spinning wool or cotton, the rovings being further drawn out as they are spun into yarn. Department 5, doubles or twists two or more threads of silk together or even a thread of silk with one of wool or other material to produce a mixed yarn. The yarn has now been spun and twisted but is not usually regarded as finished since it is somewhat 'hairy' or fluffy. This is removed in the Gassing room 6, where the yarn is passed several times at high speed through flames from gas burners. In 7, the Winding room, the yarn is first passed through Clearers, a process sometimes known as Knifing, to remove neps, slubs and spinners' piecings (terms used for unevennesses or impurities in or on the yarn), then reeled into hanks for dyeing, or wound on to cone or 'cheese' for the weaver, or washed and bleached and made into warps according to customers' orders. The Knifing process cleans the yarn and leaves it with a firm, smooth and lustrous finish. It is then passed to the Yarn Warehouse 8, where it is sorted and packed for despatch or stored.

The difference between spun silk yarn and nett silk is simply that nett silk has been made by 'throwing' or twisting together very long and fine filaments, and spun silk is the result of twisting many very short filaments of the same material. Because of this, spun yarn has tiny air pockets giving it a much warmer 'feel' than nett silk, which is cold to the touch. The average length of 1st drafts of these short filaments is six or seven inches, which is longer than those of cotton (maximum $1\frac{7}{16}$ in. staple) or even of wool, giving greater strength than the yarn of those materials. Silk filaments are finer, and the combination of fineness and longer staple length enables much finer yarns to be spun than from cotton or wool. A former long-service employee notes that spun yarn of a like count produced by different spinners might be expected to be indistinguishable, but Charles Ford, when examining a mixture of yarns from different mills would always be able to say 'This is our yarn'. He knew in some way by the 'handle'.

Ford, Ayrton washed and bleached a good deal of its yarn and sold it bleached and unbleached, but it never itself carried out dyeing. Yarn was dyed to the firm's orders immediately before 1939 by G. W. Oldham & Co. of Netherton near Huddersfield. After 1946 the work was done by J. W. White & Son (incorporating G. W. Oldham) of Macclesfield, and by Joshua Wardle Ltd of Leek, and later by Brocklehurst-Whiston (now Brocklehurst Fabrics Ltd), Hurdsfield Mills, Macclesfield. Accuracy in dyeing is always difficult to obtain and it was a constant problem with silk yarn, for which there were many obvious reasons. As already noted, raw waste silk varied greatly in condition and quality, and yarn made from silk coming from one part of the world could give a different result, even though dyed in the same way, from yarn made from silk from a different source. There are other reasons for variation in the end-result of dyeing, and occasional dissatisfaction of customers because of slight variation in shades was one of Ford, Ayrton's chief problems — as it is a problem of all firms supplying any dyed yarn. As an example of the meticulous care taken by the firm the following extract is given from the Ford, Ayrton booklet *Spun Silk Yarns*, No. 7, July/September 1936 which is on the twisting or doubling department: 'Some yarns which we have tested suggest that the makers treat their doubling department as the Cinderella of the concern, not realizing the paramount importance of absolute regularity in twist. Twist that is "near enough" may escape the eye of a casual examiner, and yet materially alter the properties of the fabric into which it enters. It may cause irregularity in count, elasticity, lustre, dyeing properties, shrinkage, etc., and hence waviness in the cloth which is sometimes attributed to other causes.

'In the matter of regular twist our aim is nothing short of mathematical precision. In the first instance we elaborated quicker and more scientific methods of testing than the time-honoured ten-inch hand twist tester, which takes no account of yarn tension, or of the (sometimes considerable) alterations of length which takes place on twisting.

'Numerous tests having convinced us that only by installing the most up-to-date twisting frames could consistent results be obtained, we decided to scrap all the old machines which had hitherto been considered quite satisfactory. This replacement programme is now almost complete, and the majority of our yarns are twisted on machines which are the latest products of the machine makers' art. Even new machines can give bad work if not operated under the right conditions, and we find it necessary to apply regular tests to the rollers and spindles — preferably under full load running conditions (which condition incidentally precludes the use of the ordinary tachometer).

'When working to close limits seemingly minor points become of importance. To give one instance, marked irregularity may be introduced into low twist yarns by lack of attention to the method of unwinding from bobbins, whether by pulling the bobbin round on a peg, or by looping over the end.

'It is quite true that, in the nature of textile materials, absolute uniformity is unattainable. Nevertheless, only by aiming at perfection, can we hope to raise still higher the reputation of excellence already enjoyed by Bentham spun silk yarns.' We believe that while this quotation is substantially true, in one point at least it is to some degree only a statement of intent, for a few of the old twisting machines were not replaced.

Waste silk was, for centuries, treated as waste. Its commercial spinning is a relatively modern development. A little was almost certainly combed and spun in early times by peasants using distaff and spinning-wheel, and this practice is still found in India and elsewhere in the East. Indeed 'Man first pulled apart the filaments of perfect cocoons for spinning . . . before hitting on the idea of reeling the continuous fibre. As a textile raw materialk silk waste may, therefore, be considered to be older than reeled silk' (*CIBA Review* — Book List 7). As already noted (p. 6) commercial waste silk spinning in Britain apparently began just before 1800 (Warner, pp. 425, 148, 402–7 — Book List 63; *Filaments* p. 8 — Book List 17). Silk throwing had been established much earlier. Spinning made little progress until after 1850, but had reached a prosperous state at about the time when Benson Ford started his business. The firms were mostly in the West Riding and Lancashire, particularly in and around Brighouse, between Bradford and Huddersfield, 'the chief centre of the English silk-spinning industry' (Warner, p. 247; *Filaments*, p. 10).

According to Warner (p. 424) there were 24 silk-spinning concerns in England in 1870, in 1886 there were 30 but the number had dropped to 24 in 1904. They were not the same firms as those of 1870: indeed only nine of those were still going even in 1886. Warner (p. 424) notes in 1921 that 'although

the trade as a whole is larger than ever, its path is strewed with
the wrecks of fallen firms': between 1870 and 1904 there were
17 failures and 11 voluntary stoppages (Iredale and Townhill,
Book List 47). The hazardous nature of the trade was largely
due to extraordinary fluctuations in the prices of raw silk which
showed variations of up to 700 per cent in the forty years before
1905. And for this and other reasons there have always been
gloomy prophets about the trade: so in 1887, Samuel Cunliffe
Lister (later Lord Masham) a pioneer and inventor in silk spinning, could say 'It (silk waste) all goes abroad, where all our
trade will eventually go. Long hours, cheap labour, and hostile
tariffs will tell more and more as time goes on' (Warner, p.
412). In 1921 there were 22 mills spinning waste silk in England
(Warner, p. 429): by 1937 there were 12 and in 1939 there were
about 10, a number which according to the *Census of Production*
had fallen to eight in 1954 and to five in 1963. There were two
in 1969 and one, Ford, Ayrton in 1970. That was the last mill
in Britain which had silk spinning as its main business — it did
occasionally spin a little man-made fibre — and which carried
out the whole process. Messrs William Thompson & Co.,
Galgate, near Lancaster, who had, for some years before 1970,
given up silk spinning except as a small side-line, continued a
part of the process for a short time by using a single frame to
spin imported silk laps. When, early in 1971, they gave this up,
silk spinning in Britain finally came to an end. William Thompson & Co. were the oldest silk spinning mill in Britain, having
started in 1793, and at the end of their career were probably
the oldest silk spinning mill in the world (*Filaments* — Book
List 17; Iredale & Townhill — Book List 47).

It is worth remarking here that the English silk spinners
were a friendly community. To some extent they were com-
petitors but they were also friends. There was outstanding
co-operation between all members of the Silk Spinners
Association.

Uses. Silk, one of the loveliest of all materials, is often
termed the 'Queen of the Fibres', and spun silk has a delightful

lustre and softness. It also has exceptional strength and elasticity and so is very durable. Garments made from it combine warmth, lightness, beauty and strength and in all weathers and climates are the most comfortable material next to the skin.

Spun silk produced by Ford, Ayrton was chiefly used for:

Knitted underwear, either silk or silk blended with wool;

woven material for *shirts and pyjamas*; *dresses and blouses*; spun crêpe, much used for these fabrics, is made with a spun silk warp and nett silk weft commonly known as 'Macclesfield silk';

Suitings: worsted and woollen cloths incorporating spun silk either as blended yarns or with some silk threads in warp or weft. Cloths were also made entirely of spun silk or more often of spun silk blended with wool, and were very popular in the U.S.A. Then there is the use of spun silk yarns as *effect threads* on men's and women's suitings. This is old established and well known, a favourite example being the white pin stripe with grey, black or navy blue background. *Fabrics* of many kinds — linings, dress materials, ecclesiastic, academic, court, legal, etc., robes and cloths, and furnishing fabrics. *Handkerchiefs, ties and scarves,* sometimes made from Tussah or 'wild' silk. *Sewing and embroidery* threads. This is a major use of spun silk yarn which is used for sewing all kinds of clothing and footwear. It is also much used for badges, braiding and embroidery. *Hand knitting yarns.* As with machine knitting, spun silk is widely used alone or mixed with wool.

Industrial uses. Spun silk was used for insulating electric wires and cables (now done by plastic material) and for weaving industrial belting, and for the bags for propellant charges from big guns and for parachute cloths and cords.

The mill's sources of power have already been mentioned (pp. 18–19). There was probably nothing in the plant which differed greatly from that used by other silk spinners; but reference should be made to that in the dressing room. Charles Ford says that a notable achievement about 1900 by Edward

Wilkinson and Benson Ford was the designing and building in the mill of the 'Transfer' dressing machines. Instead of flat dressers taking six drafts, the strippings from third drafts were taken to these unique new machines worked by women. The important new feature, Charles adds, was the nipping of the boards by hydraulic pressure, oil was used in the pump driven by an eccentric from the shafting. A subsequent improvement, suggested by Harold Warner, was made by duplicating the press, so that while one was dressing, the other could be emptied. This was used until the early 1930's when Mr Metcalfe of Clayton Metcalfe & Co., Halifax, showed Charles the Mann's Circular Dressing Machines imported from Germany. Charles always thought this a most generous action by a competitor for he was most impressed with the machine which certainly cheapened output and in his opinion improved the quality of the dressed silk. One or two of these machines with filling engines were immediately ordered and flat dressing was eventually abandoned; and this, in Charles's view, greatly increased the prosperity of the mill. This seems to have been the general view in the mill, but some had doubts. Tom Bownass, while agreeing that output was increased, says that there was a certain loss of the spirit of craftsmanship by the dresser. The flat dressers considered themselves craftsmen and indeed at one time served a five-year apprenticeship and the qualified dressers wore hard hats. They examined each board of dressed silk individually and picked out imperfections. In circular dressing the silk was removed from the opened sections of the frame in a flag and the actual dresser had no further sight of it. Girls picked over the contents of each flag in quantities containing as much silk as six dressing boards would have done. Consequently more imperfections escaped notice and more clearing was necessary in the winding room.

Circular dressing had been used on the Continent since before 1900 and Rayner, p. 92 (Book List 54) records its disadvantages; but, as we have said, the general view at Ford, Ayrton was that these were outweighed by the gains.

5

Business history

Employees, wages, hours, profit and loss, profit-sharing figures

THE FIRM was started entirely as a private enterprise by Benson Ford, joined in 1870 by William Harvey who left the business in 1877 when it moved from Leeds to Bentham. Benson Ford carried on alone until 1888 when, needing more capital, he was joined by Edward Ayrton. This private partnership was continued until 1909 when the business was turned into a Private Limited Liability Company with a nominal capital of £40,000 in £1 shares. Records of shares actually issued are: 18,761 (1909); 27,265 (1919); 27,852 (1920); 28,167 (1921); 28,210 (1923); 28,280 (1924); 28,336 (1946); and 28,346 (1947) which was the maximum ever issued and paid up. The firm's titles were:

1870–1887	Ford & Harvey
1877–1888	Benson Ford & Co.
1888–1909	Ford, Ayrton & Co.
1909–1970	Ford, Ayrton & Co., Ltd

In 1909 the legal formalities connected with the formation of the Limited Company, including the Memorandum and Articles of Association, were drawn up by Gervase Ford, of Ford & Warren, Leeds. There were to be not less than two or more than five Directors — a maximum which was increased to eight, with the introduction of Employee Directors, in 1919. For a list of the Directors and Secretaries see Appendix I, pp. 67–8.

The rest of this chapter deals with: 1. Number of employees, hours of work, wages; 2. Trading, profit and loss and dividends on shares, and — from 1917 onwards — profit-sharing bonuses. The period at Leeds is treated first, followed by that at Bentham. As records are not complete and methods of keeping them varied, it is not possible to give corresponding information for all the years; but it is believed that the selection given provides a reasonably accurate picture in outline over the 100 years.

Leeds, 1870–1887

There is full information on this period for numbers of staff, hours and wages but not for other matters. It is known that the firm started with spinning frames, the silk being bought ready dressed. There were accordingly no discharging or dressing departments. The first order book shows No. 1 order as being placed by Joseph Smithson & Co., Halifax, on 6 February 1870, for 50 lb. of 2/60 yarn at 21/- a lb. This was one of the most popular counts. It is a two-fold yarn having 60 hanks of 840 yds. each; that is, 50,400 yds. to the lb. Although for this period there are no records of profit and loss the firm made steady progress and had outgrown its premises by 1877.

Employees, hours of work, wages and salaries

The first wages book begins for the week ending Friday, 7 January 1871; wages being paid on the 8th. Work began on Tuesday, 3 January with two workers and ended on the 7th with ten. Of these Mrs Robinson received 6/- and Mr A. Stead £1. No details of work or hours of these two are recorded, and they were presumably persons in charge.

The others were:

Age	Name	Hours worked	Rate per week	Week's pay
15	Sarah Eleanor Cliff	40	6/6	4/4
13	Amelia Anne Cliff	40	5/-	3/4
13	Elizabeth Jane Granger	25½	5/-	2/2
13	Polly Bateman	25½	5/-	2/2
32	Mary Elliwell	8½	6/6	11d.
14	Sarah Ann Schofield	10½	5/-	11d.
15	Mary Ann Dawson	4½	5/6	5d.
16	Clara Gelder	7	6/6	9d.

Hence the eight workers were together paid 15/– and with Robinson and Stead this meant a total wages bill for the first week — not a full week — of £2. 1. 0. The payments show that the top rate per hour was 1⅛d. and the minimum 1d., and that working hours were 60. Next week Helliwell and Dawson had gone and there is no mention of Robinson and Stead, but they may have been paid separately. Four more girls, aged 13, 13, 16, 19 are employed; there are two weekly rates, 6/6 and 5/–, and working hours are 6 on Saturday and 10½ other days, or 58½ for the week. Nearly a full week was worked by all and the wages bill was £2. 13. 4. After this development was rapid. In February there were 20 employees and 35 by the end of March. There was no work over Easter, 8 April (Saturday), 10, 11, and no pay. By 18 February hours had gone up to 7 on Saturdays and were 59½ in the week, and weekly rates were from 5/– to 7/–. There was unpaid holiday on 25–6 December and from 2 December onwards Saturday hours were back to 6. From that time until the end of the period in Leeds the wages, hours and staff for the first week in January each year were:

	1872	1873	1874	1875	1876	1877
Weekly rates lowest	5/–	5/–	4/6	4/6	4/6	4/6
Weekly rates highest	10/6	10/6	17/–	20/–	20/–	20/–
Weekly hours	58¼	53½	53½	56¼	56¼	56¼
Total staff	41	33	34	43	56	56
Total wages	£13. 15. 11	£8. 8. 3	£9. 14. 4	£14. 8. 0	£17. 7. 8	£19. 2. 11

The hours seem to have been 10 on each day, Monday to Friday and varied from 3½ to 8½ on Saturdays. Fines, for unspecified reasons, first appear in February 1871. They are infrequent and are usually of 1d., the highest recorded being of 6d. Premiums, also for unspecified reasons, perhaps for good work or overtime, first appear against S. E. Cliff, for 2d. for the week ended 12 May 1871. They appear frequently, but irregularly, against the names of about half the employees from May 1871 until the move to Bentham. The usual figure is 2d. but is only 1d. for the lowest paid workers. The final week in Leeds was that ending 18 May 1877.

Bentham, 1877–1970

Although the firm prospered it was not the kind of business in which profits were high, and there were times of great difficulty. Charles Ford has recorded that not long after the move to Bentham 'my father went through a severe financial struggle, until the day came when he told my mother that he could not keep going and would have to close the mill. A few days later an aunt died and left him £1,000 which saved the situation.' There was at least one other occasion when private funds saved the mill. Charles notes that in the slump after 1918 the mill was in serious financial trouble, but 'Part of the John Delaney Ltd. quarries at Horton-in-Ribblesdale were on land owned by my brother and myself. An unexpected offer by the quarry owners to buy this land for about £6,000 was accepted and the mill difficulties relieved.' This was presumably in 1921 when the firm lost £11,244 in the half-year ended in March, the biggest loss in any half, or even full, year in its history for which there were special reasons, the failure of a customer and the slump (see p. 46) quite outside ordinary trade.

The following statistics continue the information given for the Leeds period, but shillings and pence are omitted from the wages totals.

	1880	1881	1902	1914	1919	1929
Week ending	18 Feb.	11 May	11 Mar.	26 May	21 Oct.	26 Nov.
Lowest wage	5/–	4/6	5/6	6/6	6/4	18/–
Highest wage	£1. 19. 5	£2. 2. 11	£1. 18. 6	£1. 17. 1	£4. 2. 3	£4. 1. 0
Weekly hours	56½	56½	55½	55½	44	44
Total staff	152	176	230	218	215	165
Total wages	£83	£95	£147	£166	£326	£306

Week ending	1939 29 Aug.	1949 27 Sept.	1965 29 Mar.	1969 18 July
Lowest wage	15/-	£3. 10. 3	£4. 10. 4	£3. 9. 2
Highest wage	£4. 2. 6	£7. 13. 9	£19. 8. 0	£14. 7. 9
Weekly hours	44	44	40	40
Total staff	130	105	89	49
Total wages	£252	£435	£517	£323

It is difficult to draw conclusions from these figures. For instance the highest wage in the 1965 column is certainly abnormal and must be for some special overtime. Furthermore, in later years some of the women worked only part-time and in the early days children were employed part-time. Will Bruce, for instance, started at the mill in 1889 aged 10. For three years he worked three days, Monday, Wednesday, Friday in the mill and was two days at school. His hours in the mill were 6 a.m. to 8; 8.30 to 12.30; 1.30 p.m. to 5.30. He was paid 2/2d. a week which increased to 3/2d. after a year. He has no memory of feeling tired at the mill. He did not dislike school but liked the mill better where he had lots of fun, especially with the overlookers. Unfortunately no overlookers' comments on young Will are extant.

In February 1969 the Juvenile Wage Scale for a 40-hour week was that at 15 years of age girls began at £5 and boys at £5. 10. 0: each increased by 5/- every quarter of a year to 17½ years when the girls got £7. 10. 0 and the boys £8.

Up to 1914, where several members of a family were employed, the total pay for all the family was paid to the senior member — often the father. So, for example, if the father had earned 30/- and three daughters 15/-, 14/-, 13/-, the father would receive in one envelope, £3. 12. 0 — made up of three sovereigns and one half in gold, and two shillings, with details on how it was made up.

Trading, profit and loss and profit sharing

Export: Although there was never a very extensive export trade the firm made strenuous efforts from its early days to sell

overseas, and until the Second World War these were not
without success. Of course many of the home customers,
having turned Ford, Ayrton yarn into material, fabrics or
garments, had large export sales.

One very successful export was for a few years from about
1880 of a sewing silk with the trade name 'Kaiser Sewing Silk'
or 'Kaiser Näh-Seide'. Coloured advertising cards and labels
were printed in England and Germany and this important line
sold well, particularly in Germany, but also in other countries,
and at home.

From the 1890's at least to 1914, direct business was done
with firms in Calais, Roubaix, Armentières, chiefly through
agents O. Denquin (Calais) and with Lyons through the
firm's agents, O. Rayroud, there. At various times in that
period and later, Ford, Ayrton had agents in Argentine
(Buenos Aires), Australia (Sydney), Austria (Vienna), Belgium
(Brussels), Canada (Toronto), Chile (Santiago), Denmark
(Copenhagen), France (Paris and as noted above), Holland
(Amsterdam), Israel (Tel Aviv), Italy (Como), Norway (Oslo),
Portugal (Lisbon), Roumania (Bucharest), South Africa (Cape
Town, Johannesburg), Spain (Barcelona), Sweden (Göteborg)
and intermittent exporting went on for some years with many
of these countries.

Ford, Ayrton could not compete with Chinese, Japanese, and
Italian silk spinners and lost first its foreign trade and was
then losing its home market. But it did not give up the fight
easily in either field. Even about 1950 there were several large
orders for Spun Silk Sewings, undyed in hank form, from a
firm in Göteborg through the agent there. One large consign-
ment had to be shipped through Liverpool and a High Bentham carrier took it directly there. When his fully laden lorry
drove away Charles Ford said he thought it was the largest
single delivery to one customer ever to be sent from the mill.
In the early 1950's a big trade was done in spun Perlon to
Holland and Belgium through the agent in Brussels; and in the
1960's there were sales to Ghana.

At home the Company had agents, at least from 1927 on-wards, in Birmingham, Bradford, Chalford (Glos.), Coventry, Galashiels, Glasgow, Leek (Staffs.), Leicester, London, Maccles-field, Manchester, Nottingham, Thurmaston (Leics.), and until the early 1960's made fairly steady sales through them and to some customers directly in other parts of Great Britain.

Ford, Ayrton's best single customers were Messrs Pringle, Hawick, and Smedley, Matlock, who produced ladies' knitted underwear. By 1957 Smedley had become the leading customer and in that year Smedley, and Ford, Ayrton made an agreement whereby Smedley undertook to order all their silk yarn from Ford, Ayrton who promised to give their orders first priority. Ford, Ayrton also undertook not to sell its business without giving Smedley first opportunity to acquire it.

From a note in *Spun Silk Yarns*, 10, 1937, 7 (Book List 21) it seems that before about 1914 several customers used to place contracts of 1,000, 2,000, 5,000 or even 10,000 lb. for delivery as required, which gave assured work for months ahead: but orders gradually dropped in size and by the 1930's there were roughly twice as many orders in a given period for the same quantity of yarn as compared with the earlier days. Although a few large orders continued to be received, parti-cularly from Smedley, the necessity to seek and accept small orders must steadily have increased production and administra-tive costs throughout the mill.

Hand-loom weavers, including amateurs, were an important source of custom and the firm had extensive connexions with them. The orders were small in weight, but hand-loom weavers are more numerous than is generally realized and the aggregate of their orders was remunerative and useful because the yarn they used, being coarse in count, was less costly to produce.

Profit and Loss and Profit-sharing

No minutes exist before the Company was registered on 1 September 1909 and the first surviving balance sheet is that issued for the year ended 31 March 1920 presented to the eleventh annual meeting of shareholders on 11 June 1920. From then on there is a complete set of balance sheets, regularly issued to shareholders but not for public circulation, down to that presented at the sixtieth annual meeting on 12 August 1969 for the year ended 31 March 1969.

Tom Bownass compiled statistics from September 1919 to March 1953, and these, continued to March 1969, give the following figures for that whole period:

Net Profits	Dividends	Share of Profits to Employees	Profit-Sharing Bonus on Dividends	Pension Fund	Benefit Fund
284,386	10,420	109,310	6,150	29,375	3,243

These figures speak for themselves. They show that over the fifty-three years the average yearly net profit was about £5,366 and the average yearly amount given directly to employees was about £2,062. But employees who were shareholders also received not only their dividends but their profit-sharing bonus on these dividends. As explained in Chapter 6 the share of profits to employees was in proportion to earnings. And even with this the above figures do not tell the whole story of what was handed to employees. Special bonuses were also paid in some years to workers in certain departments who had been on short time, and there were also the firm's contributions to the thrift fund mentioned in Chapter 6.

The period 1917 to September 1920 was reasonably profitable, but the half-year from then to March 1921 saw the extraordinary loss of £11,244 which was reduced to £5,929 for the whole year as a profit of £5,315 had been made in the first half. This loss was not due to normal fluctuations of trade. Because of the slump some customers could not take deliveries of yarn at the high prices for which they had contracted. In order to keep friendships and customers Ford, Ayrton agreed to cancel contracts and bear the loss. There were small losses in half years in 1925 and 1927 but no further loss for a whole year until March 1931 when the deficit was £2,126. This was followed by small profits until March 1935 when there was a loss of £325 for the year. Trade was then fairly good until March 1943 which showed a profit of only £1,354. This improved to £3,211 in 1944 and then for seven years there was a boom. The following figures are for the years ending 31 March. The dividend on shares was the maximum of 6 per cent and the ordinary dividend was £850 for each half-year:

	Profit	Rate	Profit-Sharing Bonus Amount to Employees	Amount on Dividends
1945	9,508	20%	3,461	276
6	10,865	40%	6,261	493
7	15,002	40%	9,634	680
8	23,736	50%	14,315	850
9	9,313	25%	7,665	426
1950	8,117	15%	5,345	234
1	8,865	20%	6,471	340

Those were the halcyon days. In the second half of the next year there was a loss, but a profit for the whole year at March 1952 of £3,309. March 1953 showed a loss for the year of £1,494. Then business again improved and was very good from 1955 to 1957 and from 1960 to 1965. In 1966 there was a reasonably good profit of £5,696 but then business rapidly deteriorated. Previously there had never been a loss in two consecutive years, but in 1967, 1968, 1969 there were losses of £936, £1,300, and £5,028. Annual sales in lb. weight of spun yarn were at March 1965, 49,835; 1966, 40,909; 1967, 32,257; 1968, 29,134; 1969, 24,193; and accelerating fall in orders showed that there would be a much heavier loss in 1970. A main reason for this was the increase in wages: this made increase in the price of yarn unavoidable and naturally caused further loss of sales. And so, for these reasons and others given in Chapter 7, it was reluctantly decided that the mill must close.

In 1947 there were 105 employees, 111 in 1952, 89 in 1965. There was a drop to 72 in 1966 and this, with little variation, remained steady until May 1969 when there were 69. On 4 July 1969 there were 55, on the 18 July there were 49, and this number then rapidly decreased with the running down of the mill.

6

Social history

BY 'SOCIAL HISTORY' is meant profit-sharing, co-partnership, sickness benefit, pension and thrift funds, holidays with pay, working hours and conditions; anything done for the employees and to bring them in to the running of the mill. Something has been said on this already, particularly in outlining Charles Ford's objects and achievements. While unnecessary repetition is to be avoided, it must be emphasized that to Charles and all members of the Ford family the all-important thing was the spirit in which and the purpose for which these things were done. They were done simply and solely because they were right in plain social justice; and to ensure that all who worked in the mill had what was due to them as of right. Charles himself repeatedly emphasized these motives and said that only on such a basis could co-partnership and profit-sharing succeed in any business. He warmly and publicly supported trade unionism which he referred to as 'the workers great safeguard' (Pitman's *Dictionary*, p. 689 — Book List 33), but was well aware of hostility to such schemes by trade unions, and fully appreciated why this should be so. If workers only in a few factories became part owners and were better off than their fellows elsewhere they might well, for example, be less inclined to join a union-organized strike, or even to use trade union machinery for bargaining, since they would have their own: they would, in short, be divided in their loyalties, and might become lukewarm in loyalty to the trade union. But Charles thought that this was mistaken in being a narrow and short term view, for 'What is good for individuals will ultimately be good for all and in the long run help trade unionism' (Pitman's *Dictionary*, p. 689). He wanted profit-sharing and co-partnership to be general in industry. And the 'good' was in the motive at Ford, Ayrton, to recognize every man and woman as an individual with personality and rights, and to be respected and treated as such: this came first and was logically followed by recognition that everyone in the firm had the right to share in the firm's profits, and, as far as was administratively possible, to be kept informed of the firm's policy, finances and trading activities and to have representatives who shared in the control of these. Charles thought that industrial friction, mistrust and unrest were largely due to workers being kept in the dark about their firm's affairs, and especially about its financial position. He strongly advocated complete frankness in all things, including financial matters: his belief was in true democratic management in industry, and that is what he strove to achieve in his firm.

A long-service former member of the firm says that Charles Ford excelled as Chairman of the half-yearly and annual meetings and these functions were much looked forward to. In earlier years all important figures — for raw materials, orders, production, sales, finances, etc.— were written on a blackboard. Later they were, of course, duplicated with the agenda sheets for all present. Charles would expound the figures and the whole trading position, giving a report on the year and discussing prospects. 'If anyone felt a bit down his personality keyed you up. That at any rate was my experience and I am sure others felt the same.'

In a letter of 8 November 1937, the Headmaster of Leighton Park School warmly thanked Charles for an address he had given to the school the previous night and added, 'It was one of the finest examples I have heard of Christian teaching being put into practice'. Charles had apparently spoken on 'What is right is possible' and the headmaster said he had long been trying to put that neatly into Latin for the school motto. It was certainly one of Charles Ford's mottoes. The guiding spirit behind his actions is perhaps even better expressed in words taken from his account of the firm's scheme to the Skipton Adult School: 'These things cannot be done without sacrifice, not only material but also the love of power over other men's lives which is in all of us. The feeling of complete ownership must give way to a sense of sharing in all things' (*Co-Partnership*, December, 1928, p. 13).

This is no place for an history of profit-sharing and co-partnership. William Wallace, *Co-partnership examined* (Book List 62), says that he does not know when profit-sharing first began: nor can any of us, for probably some form of it has always existed. Whenever the term was first used, the practice of sharing profits among those engaged in production must be old and widespread. Wallace cites one authority as giving the start in 1840 with a firm in Paris, and another putting it at 1794 with one in Pennsylvania. At all events although profit-sharing, sometimes followed by co-partnership, has spread, it has done so very slowly: it is found in many European countries, particularly France, Germany, and Britain, and in the U.S.A., but still affects only a small part of industry.

At the beginning of the nineteenth century the remarkable Welshman, Robert Owen, first at New Lanark in Scotland and later at New Harmony in the U.S.A., had introduced his schemes which included forms of profit-sharing. In England, Henry Briggs, Son & Co. of Whitwood and Methley Collieries, Yorkshire, started profit-sharing in 1865; the Southern Metropolitan Gas Company followed in 1889 and the practice was widespread in the gas industry until that was nationalized on 1 May 1949. One of the earliest textile firms to start profit-sharing was that of J., T. & J. Taylor, woollen manufacturers, Batley, Yorkshire. This began the practice in 1892 and by 1965 the major part of the firm's capital was owned by the employees, who by then had received over £3,000,000 in shares of profits in addition to wages and salaries which were at least as good as those paid in any other comparable firm. The fascinating story of J., T. & J. Taylor was told by its veteran chairman, Theodore C. Taylor (Book List 59) who started the scheme and who remained Chairman until he died in 1952, aged 102. The profits were distributed in the form of shares in the company which did not carry controlling power and there was no direct employee representation on the Board, although the Board was in fact composed of men who had been employed in the firm for many years, and in that sense were employee directors.

In 1917 Ford, Ayrton first shared profits among employees but Charles did not think that this went far enough, and in 1918, with his father's approval, he put forward a scheme for organized profit-sharing and co-partnership which came into force in 1919. This was unusual because it brought both into effect at the same time and provided for employee representation on the Board of Directors. Charles often used to speak laughingly of his first announcement of the scheme which was to overlookers and other senior employees in the mill, for, to his astonishment, they left without a word and 'I went home feeling I had made a fool of myself'. But the next morning the senior overlookers came and apologized and said that he must have thought them 'daft, and worse', but their silence was because they had been so overcome by the proposals, which they accepted with warm gratitude, and to which they promised fullest support. The firm's cautious accountant shook his head when shown the plan and, a man of few words, would only say rather gloomily, 'Most unusual, *most* unusual'. Charles went, by appointment to Batley, to get the opinion of Mr Theodore C. Taylor. He disapproved and said that the scheme was 'far too ambitious', but Charles decided to proceed. And — and this is of fundamental importance — his brother Gervase and all other members of the family gave their whole-hearted support and so did Edward Ayrton. At that time they were the only shareholders, and if one of them had taken the line 'you share your profits but not mine' the whole scheme would have failed. Charles often expressed gratitude to them and especially to Gervase, who gave him invaluable support over many years.

The essence of the profit-sharing and co-partnership scheme of 1919 — on which no major variation was ever made — is given below. The obvious point was always, and for a few people necessarily, emphasized, that profit-sharing depended on the existence of a profit, that employees could share only when there was something to be shared.

The scheme provided:

1. All employees and all shareholders received a profit-sharing bonus. All employees might buy shares in the Company at £1 each, and all shareholders, even holders of one share, were entitled to attend the shareholders' half-yearly meetings. It was never necessary to increase capital to provide shares for employees. Originally some were sold by family holders and bought again by them if required. Later, shares held by employees who died or left were usually enough to meet applications from other employees.

Since a Company cannot buy its own shares a Benefit Trust Fund was set up to buy shares of any employee who left or died, if these shares at the time were not wanted by anyone else; or to buy the shares of any employee who wished to relinquish them, perhaps because he needed money. Often there were more applicants than there were shares available: on these occasions Charles Ford usually sold some of his shares. Hence traffic in shares was fairly frequent: a check through the Company's Minute Books from 1920 to 1969 shows that transfers of shares from and to workers were recorded at ninety meetings. At eighty-three meetings names of sellers and buyers are given. There were 374 buyers — not all different people — who bought 6,269 shares, an average of just under 17 shares for each individual purchase. At seven meetings at which details of the employee buyers are not given, a further 779 shares were bought. Shares were always bought and sold at par. During this period shares — not included in the above figures — were also occasionally bought by members of the Ford family if they were not wanted by employees.

2. At the shareholders meetings complete information on the trading results and the Company's financial position was

given. Thus any employee who owned even one share could have information at first hand of the Company's position.

3. Before arriving at the divisible profit, all ordinary outgoings, depreciations, income tax, reserve funds, etc., were naturally provided for.

The next charge was the dividend on share capital which was limited to a maximum of 6 per cent per annum and was not cumulative because 'During periods of bad trade the worker is the first to suffer through loss of wages due to short time. When prosperity returns lost wages are not made up. Neither should capital's "wages" be made up, as it is if the shares are cumulative' (R. C. Ford, 'Harmony in Industry' — Book List 32). There was only one class of share. The Directors then decided what percentage figure was to be used for a bonus for:

(a) Payment to employees on earnings.

This was graded by length of service. The bonus was paid on earnings to all with under 10 years' service; on $1\frac{1}{4}$ earnings to those with 10–20 years, and on $1\frac{1}{2}$ earnings to all with over 20 years. This did not apply to bonus on shares.

(b) Payment of the same percentage as bonus to shareholders on dividends.

If the profit-sharing bonus was 10 per cent then employees of under 10 years' service received 10 per cent bonus on their half-year's earnings, the next group $12\frac{1}{2}$ per cent and the last 15 per cent. If any of these employees were shareholders they also, like other shareholders, received a bonus on their dividend, so that if the dividend was 3 per cent for the half-year all shareholders received 3.3 per cent.

Charles was never entirely happy about the payment of bonus on earnings, for obviously the higher paid people came off best, although some of the lower paid might have worked just as hard for the profits of the mill. He thought that there was a case for a flat-rate bonus to all, differentiated only by

length of service (Pitman's *Dictionary*, 687 — Book List 33).
It could be argued that the higher paid worker had more
responsibility and his work ought to be doing more for the
prosperity of the mill. But it is a difficult question, and Charles
Ford's attitude is typical of his concern for the underdog.

Pension Fund and (Sickness) Benefit Fund

Allocations to these were made when required before
dividends were decided; in fact on some occasions they were
made when the firm had made no profit. Allocations were made
to the Pension Fund current account when necessary to supplement income from investments to enable pensions to be paid;
and the same was done with the Benefit Fund. Grants were made
to the Pension Fund Capital account when there were large
profits.

The Thrift Fund encouraged employees voluntarily to
authorize weekly deductions — usually 4d. — from their pay
and bonuses. The Company invested these and added 4d.
weekly; paying capital, interest and Company's contribution
to the employee when he or she left, or, in special circumstances, earlier. When a profit-sharing bonus was paid a
deduction of 10/- was made and credited to the member's
Thrift account. Withdrawals were permitted in cases of need
and these took the place of loans which the firm used to make,
and were a more satisfactory way for the employee to obtain
money. The amounts were not large, but the end payments
were most welcome. Not infrequently they helped to provide a
girl with a *dot* on her marriage.

The Pension Scheme was entirely non-contributory and was
established to supplement national pensions. Gervase Ford
drew up the Trust Deed, which was very necessary as approval
of the Inland Revenue authorities had to be gained in order
that the firm should not be charged income tax on allocations
from profits to the pension fund. The basic fund was derived
from money accumulated during the 1914–18 war from profits
which the Ford family refused to take — they had declined to

take anything beyond 5 per cent. This fund was built up from its interest and from allocations from profits and soon stood at over £20,000, all invested in dated Trustee stock. Pensions were paid from the interest and the fund was developed by further allocations from profits. All employees had normally to retire at 65 but were eligible for pensions if they retired at 60 provided they had 20 years' service with the firm. Pensions were small: 20 years' service brought 7/- weekly: this increased for every further year of service, but the maximum was only 14/-. But even this did not compare unfavourably with the Old Age Pension which in 1919 was only 10/- weekly for a single or married person, and even by 1954 was only £2 for a single person and £3.5 for a married couple. For many years the Ford, Ayrton pensions made a great difference to pensioners' lives, and even in 1969 were a useful addition to the Old Age Pension. The pension was paid to a pensioner's widow — but not to a widower — for five years after his death; and latterly, if an employee who had been at least 20 years in the firm died before retirement, whether he had reached 60 or not, the equivalent of his pension might, at the discretion of the Directors, be paid for five years to his widow.

The Thrift and Pension Funds were administered by four Trustees, two appointed by the Board of Directors and two by the employee shareholders. In the event of an employee's absence through sickness they were empowered to continue contributions to his account from Pension Funds. If he had had 20 years' service, the Directors might grant him a pension during sickness even if he or she were under 60.

The Sickness Benefit Fund was also non-contributory and built up entirely from the Company's profits. The rates of payment were 10/- weekly for a single and 15/- for a married man, and 7/6 for a single or married woman, but 11/3 for the latter if her husband was not in regular work; and 2/6 for each child under 15 or still at school. The payments were to be in addition to, and indeed were intended to augment, any other sick benefits the employee might receive. Six months' service was

needed to qualify for sickness payments and these were made for
up to three months or two years according to length of service
in the mill. The fund was administered by a committee of four
elected by the employee shareholders, plus the Managing
Director and Company Secretary. For sick employees and
pensioners the firm had a special arrangement with a convales-
cent home in Southport.

Weekly working hours were:

1871–4	60–58½
1875–?1900	56½
?1900–18	55½
1919–59	44
1960–70	40

When Benson reduced the hours in about 1900 from 56½ to
55½ he hoped that there would be no lessening of production,
but the overlookers said that this was impossible and Benson
conceded that he had been wrong to imply that workers had
not previously been giving maximum output. However the
dressers did one end less and suffered a loss of 6d. a week which
caused some dissatisfaction for a while. The big reduction in
hours in 1919 was partly due to an incident which profoundly
influenced Charles during the 1914–18 war. He used to walk
round the mill at 6 a.m. and one winter morning he saw a boy
half asleep and realized that it was wrong so to treat children,
and that 'if he had been my son, he would still have been in
bed, and so as soon as we could we changed to 7.30 a.m. start'.
As noted on p. 14, holidays with pay were introduced in 1926.

Employee Directors. Perhaps the most advanced part of
Charles Ford's scheme was provision for Employee Directors.
When employees together held 500 shares — which they did by
1924 — they could be represented on the Board of Directors
by three of their number, who must each hold twenty shares.
One of these was appointed by the Permanent Directors, the
other two were elected at a meeting of all employee shareholders. A senior employee called this meeting and voting was

by ballot. The Permanent Directors had nothing to do with the election or the meeting, and did not attend, but the presence of the Company Secretary was necessary.

The Employee Directors held office for three years and were eligible for reappointment or election, and they were each paid, originally £10 and later £50 a year, for their service as Directors. Their position was defined: 'They shall have the right to attend Directors' Meetings, and by their advice and counsel assist in the efficient carrying on of the business, but they shall not have power to interfere with the actual management of the business which shall remain in the hands of the Permanent Directors who can be five in number in accordance with the Articles of Association of the Company.' A report on the scheme in the periodical *Co-Partnership*, December 1925, p. 43, drew editorial comment which warmly approved, but said that this definition of the rights of Employee Directors 'might be interpreted in varying ways in day to day practice. It seems, however to offer an excellent path towards experiments in bringing workers on to "Boards of Directors" and especially commended the point that "outside the Board room the worker-director resumes his normal worker position".'

The definition of the Employee Directors' position was perhaps cautious; but caution, when the scheme was made in 1919, was reasonable. In fact however, the Employee Directors were, in the Board room, on equality, in voting — although votes were rarely taken — and all other ways, with the Permanent Directors.

The provision for one Employee Director to be appointed by the Permanent Directors was also a piece of initial caution. There is nothing on record about this, but it is believed that Charles and Gervase Ford envisaged the possibility — and it was surely wise to do so — that one or both of the elected Employee Directors might be incompetent on the Board, and so they made this provision whereby the Permanent Directors could also appoint one of their own choosing. In fact, however, all the elected Employee Directors were competent in the

Board room, and after the retirement in 1933 of the initial nominee by the Permanent Directors they only appointed two others, and in neither case was this due to any shortcomings in the elected Employee Directors.

The essence of all these schemes was that they were merely giving employees something to which they were absolutely entitled; they were not 'benefits' — 'the workers have an inherent right to a larger share of the results of their labour than mere wage' (Pitman's *Dictionary*, p. 686) is the constant theme running through Charles Ford's views on profit-sharing and co-partnership. But of course he, with all others connected with the administration of the firm, was also concerned — just as most firms are — to make working conditions as good as possible and to provide amenities.

In early days the land to the south of the mill was converted into garden allotments for employees, who were charged 6/– a year each, and all employees were given free fishing rights in the river; the fishing — brown and sea trout and some salmon — was good. The bridge, built in 1929 to mark the 50th anniversary of the firm coming to Bentham, greatly shortened the walk from the village to the mill, and at the same time the rose-garden was laid out, which, with its garden seats, was a beautiful and restful place for employees in off-duty periods and for members of the village at all times. It also gave pleasant employment and a little extra income to one of the firm's pensioners. The mill came to have considerable pride in its rose garden which on one or two occasions won the silver bowl for roses awarded by the local Horticultural Society. There were, of course, normal provisions such as a rest room for women, a dining-room for all with simple cooking facilities and a drying-room for employees' wet clothes. At his private expense Benson Ford had built a tennis court near the mill and had made a bathing pool in the river with a hut and diving stage. These were originally for his children but were handed over to the mill. The Fords never believed that they should attempt to exert influence on the lives of employees outside the mill, any more than employees should try to influence theirs; all persons were independent individuals with the right to be respected and treated as such. And so the Fords preferred to support as strongly as they could village social, religious, educational, sporting and athletic activities rather than to encourage their development in the mill.

The pension scheme has been mentioned. In addition to pensions, all pensioners and pensioners' widows were always sent a small monetary gift at Christmas, and from 1935 it was also the practice that everyone retiring or voluntarily leaving the mill after 20 years' service — sometimes with rather less — received a leaving present, which was normally an article to the value of £5 later increased to £10. The presentation was made at a little ceremony in the Board room which was usually an occasion for reminiscences. There are many pleasant stories of the choosing and buying of these articles, a wrist-watch, fishing rod, chair, and so on. One lady, for instance, had to be taken to Lancaster in the firm's time to try out chairs in many shops before she was suited.

The firm owned fifteen cottages in Bentham which were let to employees or pensioners or their widows at nominal rents. Of these ten were sold to the occupants a year or two before the mill closed, and at the closure the remaining five were sold to the occupants for £50 each.

7

The run-down and closure

IT NOW only remains briefly to recount the ending of the life of the mill. To say that the future had often given cause for anxiety is to say nothing that would not apply to many businesses, but the spun-silk trade, although it had had prosperous years, was always somewhat precarious (see p. 36). The first main blow came with the development of man-made fibres, which took the place of silk almost entirely for many purposes, for example, nets, fishing lines, ribbons, braidings and women's underwear and stockings — which came to be known as 'nylons' — and partially for many others too numerous to mention. Nevertheless, there remained, and probably always will remain, a steady though much reduced demand for the Queen of Fibres. But now that the sales field was so greatly narrowed, the impact of competition, and especially of foreign competition, became more severe. There was, of course, nothing new about foreign competition in itself; what was new was that it was now being waged largely by new or rejuvenated firms. It came chiefly from China and Italy. With new buildings and modern plant, silk-spinning firms in these countries were in an advantageous position, which was further strengthened if they were part of larger organizations, as many were. As far as spun silk was concerned, Chinese and Italian firms also had much easier and cheaper access to raw waste silk than had firms in Britain, and, as is well known, they could operate more economically because of lower wages, maintenance and overheads and longer hours.

As a result, in a falling world market, whereas in 1969 Ford,

Ayrton could not sell spun silk below an average of about
68/– a lb., Italy could sell similar silk in Britain at about 66/–
and China at about 53/– and this was after having paid import
duty of 11/– a lb. The figures relatively comparable had existed for
some years and this of course meant that export trade from
Britain was impossible; for where all had to pay the same duty,
as, for example, with the U.S.A., which was the best market, Italy
could undersell us by 13/– a lb., and China by 26/–. At home,
although several old customers were extremely loyal, business
was naturally falling off. Ford, Ayrton continued sales as long
as it did partly through this loyalty and partly because its yarn
was better than most of that imported. Nevertheless the
imported yarn could also claim to be pure silk, and consumers
were being compelled to buy it in preference to the more
expensive material produced by Ford, Ayrton.

The final blow came rather suddenly, for up to 1966 business
had been fairly good, but the trading figures for 1967–9 given
on page 47, tell their own tale. The firm had consultations
with its accountants, solicitors, the Board of Trade, the
Industrial and Commercial Finance Corporation and others
and obtained reports from all its agents. All agreed that there
was no future for the mill in silk spinning or, as far as anyone
could see, in anything else. Enquiries had also been made in
various quarters to see if any other firm might wish to merge
with Ford, Ayrton or take it over, but there had been no
response. Accordingly, at the Board Meeting on 8 July 1969,
all Directors being present and the firm's accountant in attend-
ance, it was unanimously decided to close the mill, and that
the running down should begin forthwith. Immediately after
the meeting all employees were assembled and were told by the
Chairman of the Board's decision. They were also told that it
was important that all existing orders should be completed and
that the run-down would take at least until the end of the year.
There were then about 55 employees and the Board wished to
give them early opportunity to obtain other work, although
any massed exodus at that stage would have been disastrous for

5*

the mill. This was appreciated by all, and the staff loyally stood by the mill until outstanding orders were fulfilled, which is further testimony to the spirit of goodwill in the firm which had been so carefully built up over the years. But Ford, Ayrton negotiated with other firms in the district and in the next few months was able to help in placing elsewhere practically all who wished to continue working.

The decision to close the mill was taken when the firm was solvent and when it could be seen that it would still be solvent at the end of any normal period of running down. The business might have continued, perhaps for another year, and still remained solvent, but that would have been a risk which no one wished to take. Ford, Ayrton had always had a good name and everyone was determined that that should not be tarnished: the firm would go into voluntary liquidation in a state of solvency when it would pay all debts in full and all shareholders at least 20/– in the pound.

The mill then ran down, closing the departments roughly in the order of the processing line. At the same time, processed yarn, raw materials, tools, plant, office equipment, etc., were sold, bills were paid and debts collected, and negotiations were opened to sell the buildings and land. After full redundancy, care was taken to see that all other due payments were made to employees. This was a complicated matter, for although there were no dividends or profit bonuses to be paid out since there was a trading loss, yet all the various funds had to be cleared. All contributed funds were, of course, repaid to the contributors: of the others, by far the largest was the Pension Fund. This was paid to pensioners and to those employed at the mill on 8 July 1969 by the Trustees in proportions calculated by the Actuary appointed in accordance with the Trust Deeds. The total realized by the sale of the Pension Fund investments was £15,202. From this was paid: To the Actuary, £262; to the Solicitor, £108; to H.M. Collector of Taxes, £1,386. 11. 1, leaving for distribution £13,445. 8. 11. This was shared as follows:

25 pensioners and 2 widows of pensioners	£7,537. 2. 6d.
Highest share	458. 8. 6
Lowest	25.18. 6
34 Women employees	3,067.16. 8
Highest	481. 1. 9
Lowest	1. 1. 9
16 Men employees	2,840. 9. 9
Highest	479. 0. 1
Lowest	3. 5. 3

All other sums which were not the result of trading or sale of mill property were gathered and distributed on the same basis and in the same proportions as the Pension Fund. The largest item was £500 given to the mill by Helen, widow of Charles Ford, for a memorial to him. Attempts had been unsuccessfully made to give this to the village for a bus-stop shelter or something similar. Tea profits and similar small amounts brought the total to £1,162. 18. 11. The highest share from this was £41. 12. 2 and the lowest £0. 5. 8. Later, a further sum of £117 was found in the Pension Fund and this was divided equally among the pensioners.

The selling of the mill was carried out mainly by Frank Ford although he had left the mill in September 1969 and was fully employed elsewhere. This was a difficult task because there were many mill properties for sale in the Lancashire and West Yorkshire area at the time, and in spite of strenuous effort the mill was not finally sold until May 1970. Unfortunately for the employment situation in the village, the mill was bought chiefly for use as a store which required few employees. But, as has been said, practically all employees who wished to continue to work found other jobs. Most of the senior staff were approaching retiring age; but whether they took new jobs or not, all left the mill with sadness.

Various industrial archaeologists were invited to see the plant but none was interested and so most of it was sold as scrap metal; but some items were sold entire, and the preservation of one very important piece of machinery gave much pleasure to everyone. This was the engine which was the major source of power in the mill. Built and installed in 1886 by Messrs Hick, Hargreaves of Bolton, it was, after constant use during 84 years, in perfect order when the mill closed. We are sure that the manufacturers would be the first to acknowledge that the wonderful service and final condition of their engine was in no small measure due to the excellence of its maintenance. Ford, Ayrton had a splendid series of engineers (see p. 19); all first-class men who took pride in their job and gave highly skilled and devoted service. Hick, Hargreaves bought the engine and presented it to the Corporation of Bolton (*Evening News*, Bolton, 28 January 1970, p. 8), who have set it up as a showpiece in one of the town's shopping precincts — formally opened on 4 June 1973 — where it stands as an impressive example of the excellence of mechanical engineering in Bolton. The engine was regarded with affection and esteem in the mill, and not least by Charles Ford, a lover of all good engineering. Few things would have given him more pleasure than to know — if the mill had to close — that his beloved engine was being preserved in this excellent way.

The heavy, responsible and complicated task of carrying through the run-down was done almost single-handed by Will Hawkins, the Managing Director. He had the help of Frank Ford until September and of Joan Parker (now Mrs Brewster), the Company Secretary, until Christmas 1969, and from then until the end, of his wife, Mrs Norah Hawkins. Building up a business is one thing: bringing one to an end is another. Each may entail similar degrees of complicated work, but the former is an exciting and hopeful task, the latter is depressing and sad in the extreme. It needs little imagination to sense the emotional stress undergone by anyone working to close a mill which until recently had been busy, happy and full, but was now idle, dreary and empty, and with no sound but those of the scrap merchants' hammers smashing machinery of which so much care had been taken. Everyone connected with the firm was sad that the closure had to be, but no one was so personally involved in the work — which was in fact the extinction of an organization under his management and of his managerial post — as Will Hawkins. Testimony has already been made to the splendid way in which he carried out this heavy, wearing task and no apology is needed for its repetition.

The closure also compelled a complete change in the career of Frank Ford. When he joined everyone hoped that his path would follow that of his great-uncle Charles and that once again there would be a Ford in charge of the mill. Frank threw himself wholeheartedly into the work of the mill, and perhaps the only consolation about its closure, as it affected him, is that he probably saw in good time what was bound to happen and was reconciled to make a re-start elsewhere.

The last of the office staff left at Christmas 1969 and the last of the girls in the mill on 13 February 1970 when the last department, the winding room, closed, leaving only the head mechanic, Harold Foster and Will and Mrs Hawkins. They left on Friday, 3 April and the mill was later handed over to its purchaser. The Declaration of Solvency had been signed on 2 March 1970, and on 7 March, Mr Walter Denham of Messrs Atkinson, Smith & Atkinson of Leeds, was appointed Liquidator. Mr Denham had acted for his firm as Ford, Ayrton's accountant. He completed his task and issued the Liquidator's Statement of Accounts on 27 August 1971 showing that Ford, Ayrton had been able to pay its shareholders — that is, all holding shares on 8 July 1969 — 28/- for each £1 share. These accounts were approved at the last general meeting of the Company on 10 September 1971 when it was also resolved that the Company's books and documents should be transferred to the Leeds City Archives.

THE COMPANY'S PARTNERS, DIRECTORS AND SECRETARIES

THE FIRM was founded as a private business in 1870 by Thomas Benson Pease Ford. In 1909 it was turned into a Private Limited Liability Company. The senior partner and managing proprietor 1870–1909 was Benson Ford, and he was alone from 1877–88. He had in partnership 1870–7, William Harvey; 1888–1909, Edward Ayrton; 1905–9, Rawlinson Charles Ford (who had been in the firm 1897–9 and from 1902 onwards).

When the firm became a Private Limited Liability Company in 1909 the Articles of Association provided for a minimum of two and maximum of five Directors. There were four original Directors and the Board had power to appoint to the maximum number. By alteration to the Articles in 1919 the maximum number of Directors was increased to eight of which five were to be known as Permanent and three as Employee Directors. Of the latter, two were to be elected by the employee shareholders of the firm and one appointed by the Permanent Directors. Permanent Directors had each to hold at least 500 shares in the Company and Employee Directors at least 20. In the Board Room there was no differentiation between Directors.

Marked as P or E, the Company's Directors were:

Benson Ford
      (Chairman and Managing Director, 1909–18)   P
Edward Ayrton, 1909–26 (Secretary, 1909–19)   P
Charles Ford, 1909–64
      (Charman and Managing Director, 1918–64)   P
Harold Warner, 1909–13   P
Gervase Ford, 1919–63   P
Robert S. Ayrton, 1921–5 (Secretary, 1919–25)   P
Frederick Crossley, 1924–33   E
William J. Bruce, 1924–46   E
Adam Wallbank, 1924–6   E
William Lockwood, 1926–9   E
Herbert Ramskill, 1929–45   E
Robert Forrester, 1931–59   P
Albert E. Wilcock, 1944–54   E
Alexander Wilcock, 1946–52   E
William Hawkins, 1949–70
      (Secretary, 1954–64, 1970)   E (1949–56)
      (Managing Director, 1964–70)   P (1956–70)
Armistead Thornber, 1952–70   E
R. Stanley Ellershaw, 1954–62   E
Ursula O. Ford, 1959–70   P
James L. Hosfield, 1962–70   E
Elizabeth R. Pafford, 1963–70   P
John H. P. Pafford, 1963–70 (Chairman, 1964–70) P
Frank L. Ford, 1966–70   P

The other Company Secretaries were:

Thomas Bownass, 1925–54
Joan Parker (now Mrs N. Brewster), 1964–9

APPENDIX II

BOOK LIST

This is not a subject bibliography but only a list of the chief
works used in preparing this account of Ford, Ayrton.

1. Armitage, Lloyd (of William Thompson & Co., Galgate):
   The production of spun silk yarns. *Journal of the Textile
   Institute*, 26, 1935, 247–62.

2. —— Spun silk production. *J.T.I.*, 47, 1956, 785–7.

3. Berisfords, the ribbon people. The story of 100 years 1858–
   1958. pp. 81. York (1958).

4. Brocklehurst-Whiston. The story of its activities. pp. 64.
   3rd edition, Macclesfield, etc., 1952. (The firm is now
   called Brocklehurst Fabrics Ltd.)

5. Cansdale, C. H. C.: Cocoon silk. A manual. Pitman, 1937.

6. Chambers's Encyclopaedia, 1966, Vol. 4. 106–7. Co-partnership
   and profit sharing. By J. H. Richardson.

7. CIBA Review. No. 111. Spun silk. (By R. Traupel.) Basle.
   Aug. 1955, pp. 4013–52.

8. Coleman, D. C.: Courtaulds, an economic and social history.
   2 vols, Oxford (1949) (especially Vol. 1).

9. Co-Partnership. Journal of the Industrial Co-Partnership
   (*now* Participation) Association. *The following references are to
   notes on Ford, Ayrton*: Dec. 1925, 43; Dec. 1926, 21; Dec.
   1928, 13; Dec. 1930, 3; Dec. 1931, 15; Nov. 1940, 6;
   Sept./Dec. 1946, 15; Dec. 1951, 13; April, 1961, 21;
   April 1964, 18, 33.

10. Co-Partnership, etc., July 1956. This number contains 'Profit-
    Sharing and Co-Partnership Schemes' reprinted from
    Ministry of Labour Gazette, May 1956, and other articles,
    including a reprint of 'The ladder of co-partnership' by
    Sir W. H. Lever (later 1st Viscount Leverhulme), which was
    delivered 30 Nov. 1909.

11. Dyke, Millicent Zoë, *Lady* Hart: Lullingstone silk farm,
    1932–1955. pp. 79 (?1955).

12.   —— Lullingstone silk farm, Limited, 1956 and onwards. pp. (16) (?1957).

13.   —— So spins the silk worm, etc. pp. xii, 165. London, 1949.

14.   Encyclopaedia Britannica. *Articles* Silk and Sericulture, Silk Manufacture (*including* 'The spinning of silk waste'), Silk Trade.

15.   English, W.: The textile industry. Longmans (1969). Especially pp. 135–41. *See also* item 57.

16.   Fawcett, Raymond: Silk; where does it come from? P. R. Gawthorn Ltd, London (1947).

17.   Filaments, XXIII, no. 1, Dec. 1956, 7–10, '164 years of silk spinning. William Thompson & Co. Ltd'.

18.   Ford, Ayrton & Co. Ltd: Employees Handbook. pp. 28 (1965).

19.   —— Employees profit sharing scheme. pp. 8 (?1919).

20.   —— Profit-sharing in practice. A brief outline of the profit-sharing scheme of Ford, Ayrton & Co. Ltd. pp. 4. (Industrial Co-Partnership Association, London, 1949.)

21.   —— Spun Silk Yarns. No. 1, Jan./March 1935 . . . Series 4, no. 1, Sept. 1957. (These pamphlets, about 15 × 10 cm., averaging about 12 pp., were originated and largely edited by Tom Bownass. In all, 22 numbers appeared, 10 in the 1st series 1935–7, 7 in series 2 1937–40, 3 in series 3 1948–51, and 1 in series 4. They contain illustrated notes on technical processes and on Ford, Ayrton, and miscellaneous articles and poems.

22.   —— White, Fabian: Waste silk spinning. *Town and Country News*, 8 April 1927, 24–5. (Illustrated article on Ford, Ayrton.)

23.   —— Local Industries. 6 — Silk spinning at Low Bentham. *The Westmorland Gazette*, 6 June 1931 (an excellent illustrated article.)

24.   —— Workers help to run a silk mill. *Yorkshire Evening News*, 15 June 1933, p. 6. Illustrated.

25.   —— Bentham silk firm change to 40 hour week. *Lancaster Guardian*, 5 August 1960. Illustrated.

26.   —— The kindly king of employers. *Evening Post*, Leeds, 12 June 1962. (Full page on Ford, Ayrton. Illustrated.)

27. —— Guest, John: The Undivided. How success came to the house Charles built. *Evening Post*, Leeds, 25 July 1966. (Two-page article on Ford, Ayrton. Illustrated.)

28. —— Thomson, A.: Closure of one of Britain's last silk-spinning mills — Ford, Ayrton. *Journ. of Soc. of Dyers and Colourists*, 86, February 1970, p. 84.

29. —— Maynard, Bob: Bentham firm closes. *Lancaster Guardian*, 20 February 1970. Illustrated.

30. —— Pioneer partnership. *The Friend*, 15 May 1970, 564. (On R. C. Ford and the closing of Ford, Ayrton.)

31. Ford, R. C.: Address on the Ford, Ayrton co-partnership, etc., at the Yorkshire Conference of Labour Co-partnership Association, Leeds, 19 Sept. 1926. The speech was widely reported, e.g.: *The Times*, 20 Sept. 1926. Report and Leader, 'Co-partnership in Industry'; *Manchester Guardian*, 20 Sept. 1926, 'A share in profits and in control'; *Yorkshire Post*, 20 Sept. 1926, 'Co-Partnership in practice'; *Daily News*, 25 Sept. 1926, 'The worker's share'; *Daily Mail Overseas Textile Supplement*, 30 Oct. 1926, vii, Co-Partnership; *Co-Partnership*, December 1926, 21.

32. —— Harmony in Industry. *The Friend*, 30 Jan. 1942, 35–6.

33. —— Profit-sharing. (Pitman's Dictionary of Industrial Administration, Part 15, 1 Sept. 1928, 685–9.)

34. —— Then and now in a silk mill. *The Friends' Quarterly*, Oct. 1954, 211–13.

35. —— Obituary notices of. *The Friend*, 7 Feb. 1964, 159 (A. Raistrick); 14 Feb. 1964, 198–9 (O. Hodgkin, Gladys M. Wade, Enid M. Forrester); *Craven Herald and Pioneer*, 17 Jan. 1964; Co-Partnership, April 1964 (W. Hawkins).

36. Gaddum, P. W.: Silk: and and where it is produced. pp. 64. H. T. Gaddum & Co., Macclesfield, 1972. (9th edition. First issued in 1948.)

37. Goodale, *Sir* Ernest W.: Design and the silk centre (*J.T.I.*, 42, 1951, 857–66).

38. Gordon-Brown, Ian: The management of motivation (Co-Partnership, July 1970, 36–7).

39. —— Participation in industry: an introductory guide. pp. 56. London, 1972.

40. Hart Dyke, Zoë, *Lady*. *See* Dyke, Millicent Zoë, *Lady* Hart.

41. Hayakawa, Takuro: The raw silk industry of Japan. Japanese Silk Association, Tokyo, 1953.

42. Hooper, Luther: Silk, its production and manufacture. Pitman, 2nd edition, 1927.

43. Howitt, F. O.: Bibliography of the technical literature on silk. Hutchinson, 1946.

44. —— Silk. pp. 22. Manchester Textile Institute, 1948.

45. —— Silk; an historical survey (*J.T.I.*, 42, 1951, 339–60).

46. Huber, Charles J.: The raw silk industry of Japan. The Silk Association of America, New York (1929).

47. Iredale, J. A. and Townhill, P. A.: Silk spinning in England: the end of an epoch. (*Textile History*, 4, Oct. 1973, 100–8.)

48. Lardner, D.: Cabinet Cyclopaedia. *See* Porter, G. R.

49. Lever, *Sir* W. H. (later 1st Viscount Leverhulme): The ladder of Co-partnership, 1909. *See* Co-Partnership, July 1956. (Lever's article discusses Trade Union opposition to co-partnership.)

50. Lewis, John: The silk book. pp. 107 plus illus. and fabric specimens. London, Silk and Rayon Users' Association, 1951.

51. Pitman's Dictionary of Industrial Administration. *See* Ford, R. C.: Profit-sharing.

52. Porter, G. R.: A treatise on the origin . . . and present state of the silk manufacture. pp. 339. *Anon*. The Cabinet Cyclopaedia by Dionysius Lardner . . . Useful Arts. London, 1831. (Also issued, undated, without reference to Lardner's Cyclopaedia and with different imprint.) Makes no reference to commercial silk spinning. Gives brief mention only of waste and distaff spinning on pp. 190, 192–3.

53. Rawlley, R. C.: Economics of the silk industry. London, 1919.

54. Rayner, Hollins: Silk throwing and waste silk spinning. pp. 154. London, New York, 1903.

55. Schober, Joseph: Silk and the silk industry. Translated by R. Cuthill. London, 1930.

56. Silk Book, The. *See* Lewis, John.

57. Singer, C., Holmyard, E. J. *and others*: A history of technology. Oxford (1958). Especially Vol. IV, pp. 313–16, 321–7 on silk waste processing by W. English. *See also* item 15.

58. Spun Silk. pp. 19. Bradford. The British Silk Spinners' Association (?1936). Reissued as 'Spun Silk. A short account of its origin, manufacture and uses'. pp. 10. London. The Silk Centre (?1955).

59. Taylor, Theodore C.: J., T. & J. Taylor Ltd. One hundred years. Records, recollections and reflections. pp. 45. Leeds, 1946.

60. Taylor, J., T. & J. Taylor Ltd.: Particulars of the Company and of the profit-sharing scheme. pp. 7. Batley (?1965).

61. Thompson, William & Co., Galgate. *See* Armitage, Lloyd *and* Filaments.

62. Wallace, William: Co-partnership re-examined. pp. 61. London, Industrial Co-Partnership Association (1955).

63. Warner, *Sir* Frank: The silk industry of the United Kingdom. Its origin and development. pp. 664. London (1921).

64. Williams, Aneurin: Co-partnership and profit-sharing. London, Home University Library (1913).

INDEX

The index is selective. Works referred to and entries in the Book List (pp.69-73) are among items not indexed.